Queens Supporting Queens

An Anthology Compilation

by

Tanya R. Thompson

Queens Supporting Queens
An Inspirational Anthology
© 2020 Tanya R. Thompson

Glory After the Rain Publishing
All rights reserved.

Please note: The individual stories contained herein are protected by individual copyrights from each contributing author and their individual title listed. No parts of their stories may be reproduced or duplicated without their express consent.

Scriptures marked KJV are from the King James Version, public domain. Scriptures marked NIV are from the New International Version of the bible. © 1973, 1978, 1984 International Bible Society. Used by permission. Scriptures marked NIV are from the New International Version of the Bible. © 1965, 1987 by the Zondervan Corporation. Used by permission.

Glory After the Rain Publishing uses a publishing style that capitalizes certain pronouns in the scripture that refer to the Father, Son and Holy Spirit, and may differ from other publishing styles. Please take note that satan and other related names will not be capitalized. We have made the choice not to acknowledge him, even to the point of violating grammatical rules.

ISBN: 978-0-578-66731-7

DEDICATION

This book is dedicated to my beautiful daughter, Mikayla Thompson. You have been a blessing in my life since day one. Thank you for making motherhood an easy task for me. You are anointed and God has so much work for you to do. You are being prepared for greatness, daughter. You have felt the sting of betrayal, the winds of loneliness, and the heaviness of hopelessness at such a young age. Nevertheless, you always come out victorious! You are greater than your current set of circumstances. Keep pressing. You are a Queen. I am so proud of the woman that you are becoming. When life hands you a seemingly unsurmountable set of circumstances, simply adjust your crown as needed and go forth in victory!

With Love,
Mommy

CONTENTS

	Acknowledgments	i
Chapter 1	Think It Not Strange	1
Chapter 2	Healing the Hole in My Soul	6
Chapter 3	Reflect. Repair. Replace.	10
Chapter 4	Poetry for A Queen	18
Chapter 5	The "No" that Changed My Life	21
Chapter 6	Honoring A Queen	26
Chapter 7	My Survival Guide #1: The Big "C" is Christ	30
Chapter 8	Blessed Extractions	34
Chapter 9	Unless He Be Drawn	36
Chapter 10	Accepting the Irreversible	39

Chapter 11	Unable to Breathe	45
Chapter 12	Look at Her: A Story of Forgiveness	50
Chapter 13	Who am I?	54
Chapter 14	Knowing Who You Are	59
Chapter 15	The Hole in My Soul	61
Chapter 16	It's Your Time	64
Chapter 17	It's Our Issue, Too	69
Chapter 18	Almost Homeless…But God	72
Chapter 19	Forgiveness	77
Chapter 20	Attraversiamo	80
Chapter 21	Finding Purpose After 40	85
Chapter 22	The Power in Being Weak	88
Chapter 23	Unmasking the Authentic Queen Within	91
Chapter 24	We Are Better Together	94
Chapter 25	Women Helping Women	98
Chapter 26	Extraordinary Sisters	102
Chapter 27	The Overcomer	106
Chapter 28	Seize the Moment	110
Chapter 29	The Price of Peace & Sanity: Choose You	114
Chapter 30	The Favor of God	118

ACKNOWLEDGMENTS

I would like to thank the staff and interns of Glory After the Rain Ministries for operating in complete excellence as we worked through the challenges of my personal illness, loss and even natural disaster while working to complete this project. Thank you for your incredible faith in the vision. Without you, this would not be possible. To the ladies of the Queens Supporting Queens Anthology thank you for your loving kindness and continued support from start to finish. God has been glorified by your sacrifice and obedience during this writing process. I look forward to hearing the testimonies from women across the globe as they read your stories.

CHAPTER 1

Think It Not Strange
Tanya R. Thompson

"Beloved, think it not strange concerning the fiery trial, which is to try you, as though some strange thing happened unto you," 1 Peter 4:12

Two minutes and 34 seconds. This is the amount of time it took for our world to be flipped upside down. It moved at speeds up to 134 miles per hour and it took no prisoners. It was powerful and left its fingerprint across a 10-mile radius in the city of Nashville, TN. The culprit was a deadly tornado that met us at 1:35 a.m. on March 3rd, 2020. We would later learn that it was categorized as an EF3. We were left in the dark, confused and scared but alive.

I remember lying on the floor crying out to God to save us from death and to spare us from total destruction. It seemed that the louder I cried, the greater the intensity of the storm around us. The sound of one hundred year-old trees being ripped from their once stable foundation is a sound that I have never before experienced. The high-pitched decibels of sheet metal, roofing and the clanking of a devastating menagerie of broken glass serves as an unforgettable timestamp that will forever be etched in the corners of my mind.

The rain was pouring quite heavily and seemed to be in competition with the powerful wind gusts to gain the prize for most frightening soundtrack of destruction. All around our home there were sounds of the once beautiful homes in the area being completely torn from their foundations. The new age, modern "tall and skinny" houses that were once all the rave were now reduced to a pile of rubble. The telephone poles that stood tall and lined the streets in the neighborhood for several decades looked like giant toothpicks. The area looked like a certified war zone.

At two minutes and 35 seconds, the winds and rain ceased. An unexplainable darkness fell upon the area like a fleece blanket that is spread upon a tiny helpless newly born baby. Upon looking out the window, we noticed that we could not see even a few feet in front of us. We would not fully understand the deadly turn of events that had transpired until morning.

At the first sign of daybreak, we were astounded to see the aftermath of the devastation. Our neighborhood was reduced to large pieces of plywood entangled in tree limbs and downed power lines. It was like a rainforest in the middle of an urban district. We were trapped. There was no way in or out of our street at first glance. Watching the news was a normal occurrence each morning. However, without power this would not be in the cards for us. We were cut off from the rest of the world. You could almost say that we were unaware of the true level of devastation that had touched the remaining portions of the city.

The coming days would be a gentle reminder of the goodness of God and His loving kindness. We were showered with the love of Jesus through strangers of all ages, color, and religious background. The needs of the community were immediate and even overwhelming at times. But, the hand of God was steady and omnipresent throughout this entire ordeal.

My mother sat on the porch wrapped in a beautiful chenille blanket that was given to her by concerned volunteers. She is 67 and feisty. She loves the Lord with her whole heart, and He continued to show Himself mighty through this storm. There were several needs that mom had on her mental checklist. She did not have to make a clarion call for help. She only whispered to the Father God what she was in need of…and it was delivered! Literally. Volunteers came from all street directions by foot to bring forth any and every need that she could have possibly uttered unto God. She was blessed with a lantern that used several batteries.

While I am happy that so many basic necessities were provided during this storm, I felt an increasing sense of being overwhelmed physically, emotionally and mentally. It seemed that so many things were transpiring at once. My body was tired from the many months of trying to heal itself and my mind could not wrap itself around the fact that we were experiencing such great loss and devastation. Darkness fell at 6pm. I found myself within my covers, which had recently become my refuge. It was dark because of the power outage. It was lonely. But I felt myself drifting off to sleep as silent tears ran down my face. I was tired. Anxiety and depression were creeping in.

The next morning, I placed my feet upon the floor to start my day, and I was faced with a tremendous decision. I looked at my feet as they pointed downward towards my slippers at my bedside. As I gazed into the mirror by sunlight, I noticed that my once long and healthy hair had become thin and brittle. My skin felt dry and unkempt. I noticed that my posture had changed of late. I had started to sit up in bed with my head held down and my shoulders slumped forward; almost as if I am forfeiting the fight without even trying to win. This is not customary for me. I am known for proclaiming, "This is the day that the Lord has made. Let us rejoice and be glad in it!"

But, to be honest I did not feel a sense of joy. My sense of peace had been replaced with fear and uncertainty.

At this point, my personal health status has been extremely unpredictable for the last 186 days to be exact. Yes, I counted. And within those days, I have found myself questioning my faith and my purpose in God. I have reflected over my life and the numerous ministry assignments that God has placed in my path and I wonder why I am able to pray heaven down on behalf of others and they are healed; but some days, I am so sick that I don't even have the strength to hold my head up. I wonder why I am able to pull from the scriptures and counsel others effectively, but when I need pouring into, I have no one.

On this day, I had to make a choice. I had to choose between premature death and the continuation of my life; even if the circumstances that surrounded my life were strange and seemingly unfair. The storms of life had left abrasive scars due to the unrelenting winds and rains that poured upon me. I am tired of being sick. I am tired of hospitals, blood tests, advanced imaging studies and the constant cancellation of previously planned events because of my extended illness. I am 43 years old and single, without a prospect for a mate in sight. There is no shoulder that I can cry on in the midnight hour when things become hard to bear.

My heart, lungs and kidneys have been on a journey that I would not wish on my worst enemy. "Nevertheless, God is faithful. I *must* believe this to be true." This is what I reminded myself as I sat on my bedside contemplating ending it all. I remember asking God why I had to endure all these trials and tests. I wondered if anyone would even miss my presence. I figured that if I stop taking my insulin, and cease swallowing the rest of the 14 medications that I must take daily to live, that I would be much better off. I would be "normal." The house is cold and damp from the storm that had just passed. We are without heat because there is no power. "How much more must I take, God?"

As I placed my feet into my slippers and used the last bit of energy to stand up, I felt a sudden shift within the atmosphere. It was a spiritual shifting. It was as if I could feel the prayers of the righteous moving heaven on my behalf. I could hear a breaking of strongholds in the spirit.

My body was weak, and I was uncomfortable due to the drastically low temperatures, but I could feel the presence of God holding me so that I would not fall. I heard the words *"Talitha Cumi"* being whispered over and over. A single tear escaped down my face as I remembered what this phrase meant.

Talitha Cumi is an Aramaic phrase that can be found in the book of Mark 5:41. These are the words that Jesus spoke when He raised Jairus's daughter from the dead. The Aramaic language would have been the familiar language used daily during this time. If you study further, the word Talitha is used as a term of endearment. Etymologically speaking, it is related to a word that translates into "lamb."

When you think about this story and the fact that Jesus took this little girl by the hand and used this term of endearment, it shows the gentle compassion of our Heavenly Father. Though we may be facing various trials that seem unfair or hopeless, we must think it not strange. When we are being obedient and walking within our purpose, we must think it not strange. The faith that we carried when the sun was shining, is the very same faith that we must exercise during the difficult storms.

God had to remind me that a heavy mantle and a powerful anointing are not signs that you will be exempt from trouble. It is quite the contrary. To whom much is given, much is required. God was asking for more of me, but I did not understand how I could give more than what was already being given in His name and for His service.

God reminded me that I was to move into my purpose and operate under the umbrella of His power and not my own. I was totally stunned. I did not realize that I had been trying to work on a supernatural level while operating in a natural state. I am not strong enough, smart enough or big enough to make mountains move. I need the help of my Father who gives me the authority to move in His name.

I had to repent unto God. I had allowed the voice of satan to whisper death into my current events section of my life story. However, that is not my portion. God made a promise to me. He promised that I would not leave this world until the mandate and assignment on my life were completed. I was almost guilty of giving up the ghost, when God was clearly telling me to get up and live!

Think it not strange when everyone around you seems to be blessed financially, but you are paying tithes and offering, sowing seeds of time and talent and even volunteering as an extension of Christ, but it seems like those things that you have been waiting for God to release have not yet come to pass. You should not think that it is strange that you are unable to see an immediate return on your sacrifice. God is cultivating the soil in the spirit realm. When the time is right, He will release the harvest!

In the days since this natural storm, I have also started to recover from the spiritual storm. I have learned to allow only positivity to pass through my lips. There are things that I have been loosely believing God for. But now I believe with my whole heart and I allow God to show Himself in my life. I asked God to do specific thigs within my life. During this season, I know that it could only be the hand of God that has caused these things to fall into place. I refuse to think that my circumstances are somehow strange, and that God is singling me out to be tortured. This is not how He operates.

John 10:10 (KJV) reads, *"the thief comes only to steal, kill and destroy. I have come that you might have life and that they might have it more abundantly."* I have made a conscious decision to live. I declare that God will take care of my healing. I speak life to my body, and I declare that I will live. I declare that resources are coming from the north south, east and west. I believe these to be human resources (Godly connections), financial resources and spiritual resources. There is no good thing that God will withhold from me.

Queens we should think it not strange when you are faced with various trials and tribulations. No matter what you are going through, God will continue to hold you by the hand. He will whisper for you to arise and walk with Him. He will never leave you nor forsake you. Don't give up! If you are thinking about giving up, don't faint. Someone else's destiny is tied to your obedience. Remember the promises of God.

CHAPTER 2
Healing the Hole in My Soul
Evangelist Sraya Fears

This chapter was written to uplift and encourage you while offering practical insights that will point you to God. I believe this will be a chapter of hope for surviving the trauma of hurt, brokenness, bitterness and resentment. I pray that it will serve as a gamechanger in how you will look at the inner healing of your soul. Know that you are not alone because there is divine healing for you.

We have all heard of the importance of the mind, body and soul connection. Yet, most of us put our spirit, and our soul, last. This leaves us out of balance and sets us up for pain and suffering. Although positive thinking and actions are essential, we must first go to the root of our suffering which can only be found within ourselves. Don't wait until your heart and spirit have died to nourish your soul. You see, when we become a believer, our spirit is made right with God. Sometimes our soul doesn't get the notice because we have a hole in it secondary to things that have happened in our past. Events such as hurt, abuse and even molestation may have happened to you. I want to speak to you on today and tell you that God wants you to come to Him with your hurt and pain. I pray that the wisdom that I share in this chapter will help you to get over your past and remind you that God wants to heal the hole in your soul.

I am passionate about sharing my story with other women who need to experience freedom through a personal relationship with Christ and the power of God's word. For the past two years God has been telling me, "I want your testimony. Your testimony will set many free!"

In October of 2019 I started sharing my story and telling women what I had gone through and how God healed my brokenness, which gave me a life of purpose, peace, joy and real love. Long story short, approximately three years ago my marriage experienced unbelievable havoc! Talk about pain, suffering, and extreme humiliation. My heart was shattered, my soul completely crushed! I thought, "How could this happen to me?" I didn't deserve this!

Oftentimes, we think to ourselves that the past is the past and we can move on and live our lives. Yet, you are likely to find that your past doesn't just disappear as time passes. It seems that you are left alone to carry this pain of the past. God has tenderly reminded me that pain itself is not the enemy. Pain is the indicator that brokenness exists. Pain is the invitation for God to move in and replace our faltering strength with His. I am not writing this to throw out spiritual remarks or statements that sound good.

I say this from the depths of a heart that knows that it is the only way. Jeremiah 30:17 says, *"But, I will restore you to health and heal your wounds, declares the Lord."*

Most of us attempt to numb our pain with food, drugs, alcohol or sex- but the truth is, this method never gets to the real issue or source of our pain. It only silences our screaming need for help. We think that we are freeing ourselves from the pain but what numbs us imprisons us. If we avoid the hurt, it creates a hole in our soul. It slowly kills the potential for our hearts to fully feel, connect and love again. It even steals the best in our relationship with God. Jeremiah 33:6 says *"Nevertheless, I will bring health and healing to it. I will heal my people and will let them enjoy abundant peace and security."*

Before you can heal your soul, you must claim and sit in the pain and loss. It is perfectly alright to acknowledge the hurt that you have experienced. It is acceptable to cry over the sadness of the past and sit in the sorrow that you feel. Whatever holes that you may have in your soul or losses that you may have been carrying; you must allow the light, divine love, and God's Word to wash your wounds. Let's pray before we discuss the process of healing your soul.

Dear Lord, I kneel before you at this moment, I need you to heal my heart, mind, and soul and make me whole again. I have been feeling this heartache for so long and I need to move on with my life. Lord please comfort me and surround me with your peace and love. Amen.

The purpose of telling my story is to share the importance of taking care of your soul. So how can you start giving your soul the nourishment that it needs? It is not as difficult as you think. Remember that your soul is the divine aspect of you, and as such, it knows you better than anyone. It sees you as completely worthy and loves you unconditionally. Psalms 147:13 says, *"He heals the brokenhearted and binds up their wounds."*

There are three types of healing that are detrimental to the healing of your soul. They are spiritual healing, psychological healing and physical healing. I believe that spirituality's idea of wholeness into the realm of psychology and the physical can bring about transformational healing through uniting the soul, mind and body. Through Jesus Christ we can experience spiritual, physical and emotional healing.

Firstly, I believe in the spiritual perspective that this means praying and meditating no matter how vast your circumstances may be, prayer is big enough to fill us with the realization of His presence like nothing else. Healing spiritually is a process of multiple and perhaps contradictory emotions arising all at once. But have faith in your ability to heal. Have faith that you are whole and believe that this experience will pass.

When waves of anger, unforgiveness, or resentment pop up, it is easy to resist them. Surround yourself with God's divine love and His Word because the very people that you hurt will need your prayers and forgiveness. Forgiveness is not a cruel demand that a sadistic God imposes on the hurting. It is the painful but healing door to freedom. It is surgery on the heart that extracts the poison of bitterness and the loss of reward. Ephesians 4:32 says *"Be kind and compassionate to one another, forgiving each other, just as Christ forgave you."*

Secondly, is the psychological perspective. The mind is a powerful tool. You must learn to let go of things that you cannot control. Even though this is easier said than done, it is essential in healing your soul. Look deeply and honestly, perhaps going way back before the heartache, betrayal or set back occurred. As you dig into your memories, difficult feelings may arise. By triggering these difficult memories, you increase healing in the deeper parts of your soul and mind. Do not judge yourself for having painful or ugly emotions. Give yourself time to feel; no matter how long it takes.

Lastly, we have the physical perspective. Most of our pain and suffering is due to living by the negative emotions you memorized from the past. Break out of your routine. Oftentimes we find ourselves living the same routine over and over. You can break out of your routine by changing your physical environment or perhaps switching the order in which you do your daily tasks. Maybe you could change your appearance, your hairstyle or even your hair color. Perhaps you could join a fitness gym and take classes to release any anger you may have built up. Whatever energy that the situation calls for, try to tune into your inner self. Give yourself what you need. Have faith that your energy will return and your hurt, anger, unforgiveness, and resentment will dissipate allowing your soul to be healed. You have the power to move through this and learn from it. Set boundaries to prevent similar situations from happening again.

We all go through heartaches, betrayals, setbacks and things that we don't understand. Maybe you stood in faith in a marriage or relationship, but it didn't work out. Maybe you were betrayed by someone that you held near and dear, and they failed you. Maybe what you thought was a setup ended up being a setback. One of the best things you do is release it and let it go.

When you release it, this is an act of faith. The heartache, betrayal and setback may not have been fair, but it is all a part of your divine destiny.

If you will forgive, let it go and move forward, then you will come into a season of something awesome. God is about to do something that is not ordinary…but extraordinary according to God's plan!

So, continue to read the Word of God and stay in prayer so that your attention remains focused on the Lord; not the things of your past.

Once you give your soul the nourishment it needs, you will subsequently strengthen your mind, body and spirit causing your life to be more balanced, more peaceful and more joyful. Starting here and now, the things that hurt you in the past won't control your future anymore. You are officially released from what once put a hole in your soul.

CHAPTER 3
Reflect, Repair and Replace.
Pam Ryans

> *"For our struggle is not against flesh and blood, but against the rulers, against the authorities, against the powers of this dark world and against spiritual forces of evil in the heavenly realms." Ephesians 6:12 NIV*

While reflecting on the countless noticeable behaviors in todays society, I have concluded that although we may be adults, there is a child inside of us still possibly facing some form of hurt. Their hurt is stemming from the past and is forcing its unresolved emotions into our present-day livelihoods. It is being leaked down through our generations. As generations progress, families are becoming more ill, simply because the wound was never addressed, taken care of and allowed to properly heal.

Let's look at AJ. AJ is a fictional character who represents many individual's maturation into adulthood. He has a wonderful family. Yet, he is making present day choices based on yesterday's emotional scars. AJ is a divorced recovering drug addict, who is a successful business owner, seeking knowledge, seeking God and appears confident.

AJ grew up as an only child. His mother was an identical twin, divorced from his biological father. However, his aunt was unwed with three children. AJ had the privilege of playing with his cousins whenever he wanted, often demanding and dismissing playdates at his will. Once the cousins were gone home after the playdate, AJ's mom would ask from behind closed doors while she entertained her various gentlemen, "AJ are you ok?" AJ repeatedly responded "Yea. I'm ok." He wasn't. When AJ felt lonely, he would summon his cousins to play, often monitoring and controlling his toys. Then, when they seemed to be having too much fun, he would tell his mom, "make them go home."

I witnessed AJ, now 50 years old display this exact behavior with various women in his life. He summons and entertains them, only to ultimately dismiss them *at his will*. They are not aware of the disrespect with other women. Often, they feel special, but the abrupt dismissal feels a bit selfish. He's extremely kind and overly giving. He has the appearance of love but does not actually say that it is love.

Recently, I overheard a conversation between AJ and his mom. The phone rings and AJ answers.

Mom: "Hey Boop!" she says excitedly

AJ: "HEY" he says in a dragging and disturbed tone. It sounds like she's getting on his nerves.

Mom: "Are you picking me up? Do you think you have time?"

AJ: "YEA" (sighing).
Mom: "Well I got my dress and shoes upstairs. I'll be ready."
AJ: "Aight then."
Mom: "I love you."
AJ: "Aight!"
The conversation ends and he hangs up the phone.
Me: "OMG, AJ! You don't tell your mom you love her? Do you tell your daughters? Did you love your ex-wife? Did you tell her you loved her?"
AJ: I tell my girls, "Daddy loves you." I didn't tell my ex-wife; she could look in my eyes and tell. And, I took care of home. I don't tell my mom. The men in my family aren't affectionate.

Now hold on. Don't get your feathers ruffled. This is NOT a situation to judge. It is a scenario to examine. This is a person just like many of us. The enemy has planted a seed in childhood. The person is fully grown but his emotions are in seed-form. Let's reflect, replace and repair.

(Disclaimer: I am not a medical professional. This is a surface level healing. You are participating in this process at your own will and risk. If you know you need medical, psychiatric or professional assistance, seek it and get help.)

Reflect
Although scripture tells us to forget the past; we have NOT. As you take this final travel to the past and close its door, be sure to pray.

"Father God, as I revisit my past, comfort me. Protect me from the turmoil the enemy may try to cause. God, as I glance back, don't allow the enemy on this journey. Bind every attempt to sabotage my healing. I am healed. Help me God to lay my issues to rest forever. Help me realize my freedom and my healing. In the name of Jesus. Amen."

So, what's in AJ's past? His mom gave him her last, often as hush offerings to keep him away from her adult entertaining with men. His mother was a divorced single mom. AJ's dad divorced his mom, married again and now loved someone else with THEIR kids. The one person AJ loved said she loved his dad and him but showed love to other men.

Since AJ's dad was no longer under the same roof, mom would occasionally leave the back door open for her "friends." They would wait until AJ was asleep.
Often, he wasn't. When he wasn't asleep the men would give him a dollar and send him to his room. He would hear loud music and laughs.
AJ dropped out of high school and later acquired his GED. He enlisted into the military and later found the lethal cycle of habitual drugs.

Go back as far as you can remember. Play back each year, grade, instance, or moment in your mind. Allow yourself to feel the feelings of each hurtful moment. Although it may be a tragic event, allow yourself to feel the emotions. Cry, scream, or laugh. Reflect but do not cause harm to yourself. In reflection, own that the situation really happened. Face the fact that it wasn't your imagination. Now, after you've recalled this occurrence, remember it has already passed; and you made it.

Choosing to move forward is not saying that the hurt didn't happen. It says you survived to move forward. We do not have to remember what someone did *to* us in the past. We do not have to remember what we *did* in the past. It is possible to forget those things which are behind and look forward to the high calling in Jesus, which is found in love.

I will not minimize the hurt you felt. I too have had hurtful moments. I will not lie to you saying walking into the future is not painful because closing those doors, ending those relationships and cutting some folks off will hurt. However, I will PROMISE that you are never alone. Jesus HAS come to give you abundant life.

"There is therefore now no condemnation to them which are in Christ Jesus, who walk not after the flesh, but after the Spirit." Romans 8:1

What did you discover in your journey of reflection? What/Who/Where is the source of your present-day issue stemming from a past event? Identify the area of your issue. The location is within your pain. It is where you were/are most affected. The site of hurt is the location of the seed the enemy planted. Regardless of how we try to move forward without healing, the enemy continues to water the seed. His watering technique can be found in our bad choices, mismanagement of our life's worthiness, passing the curse throughout the generations, etc. It is important to identify the stolen seed, because the enemy must give it back with interest.

"But if he be found, he shall restore sevenfold; he shall give all the substance of his house." Proverbs 6:31

Repair

Reflection reveals that if you can journey backwards to your past and admit you survived, you can now move on. Right? Congratulations! You made it. Still we must pray.

"Father, thank you for saving and delivering us from the past. Help us now God to forget those things which are behind us. Help us to journey towards the future where you are. God, I thank You because You will repay all the enemy has stolen from us. In the name of Jesus. Amen."

The first, and maybe most important tool in the box, is the power to forgive. Let's pause AJ. He is in the process and doing quite well. Though painful, he is willing to revisit the past and heal. AJ's journey is a familiar story. Many can identify with the encounters of his past. It's time for me to own and share my journey.

As I lay on my sofa one evening, I had a conversation with God. I realized I was severely abused by myself and others. It was an exhaustive lifestyle. I asked God, "What is it?" He showed me. He did just as I asked. It was horrific.

The memory of things I saw in my past hurt for days and days. Still, I bravely journeyed backwards through the many episodes. Then, I asked God to identify what I saw. As He began to show me my behavior, I googled definitions and descriptions to determine the terms, titles, and words to match. I was ashamed. I couldn't believe that I behaved so poorly. Then, I owned the descriptions and titles. Then, I owned the proven textbook definition.

I was broken, but ok. There was no need in blaming anyone; not even myself. So, I thanked God that I made it through such horrible descriptions and behaviors. Next, I released it all by recalling the words of Romans 8:, *"There is therefore now no condemnation to those who are in Christ Jesus, who do not walk according to the flesh, but according to the Spirit."*

I forgave myself and others. There is no more, "How could I? I can't believe I did that." I let it go. No condemnation. Not forgiving ourselves and others keeps us bound to the past. We are chained to it. We are committing ourselves to a lifelong imprisonment. We must break the chains and free ourselves. *"Behold; God is doing a new thing. Can you see it? Now it springs forth."* Isaiah 42:9. You are a new thing. That new creation! A new creature in Christ.

Journeying backwards to my past and deciding to forgive did not happen overnight. I'm releasing this exercise to help you speed up your process. Work at your own pace. Repair the "broken you" with forgiveness.

I recall lying on that sofa night after night in anguish. I was waiting for the person they called the Holy Spirit. The One that I had raised my hands for over the years. With hands raised I was saying He lived inside of me. Clearly it was a thing I did in the "heat" of a praise and worship moment. Did I truly believe He lived in me? Because after leaving the service it appeared that He left me…or so I thought.

Replace

God instructed me to stop. Stop thinking and stop condemning myself; just stop. Then He spoke. In the calm of my entire environment without music, no children's laughter, no TV and only dim lights, this is what He said:

1. *"Trust in the Lord with all you heart and lean not to your own understanding."* Proverbs, 3:5
2. *"Casting all your cares upon Him; for He careth for you."* 1 Peter 5:7
3. *"And be not conformed to this world; but be ye transformed by the renewing of your mind, that ye may prove what is that good and acceptable, and perfect will of God.* Romans 12:2

In essence, we must replace what we say and what others say about past with the words that God/Jesus/Holy Spirit says about us. And that is, *"This is my child in whom I am well pleased."* Matthew 3:17.

We must trust the trials and events of our past as a part of a plan. The road may have veered in the wrong direction, but God is still there. If the things we did were of our own free will or not, God still works on our behalf. If someone wronged us, God is still working on OUR behalf. In order to move forward with life, we must cast our cares on the one who TRULY cares for us. His name is Jesus.

In Matthew 11:29-30, Jesus says, *"Take My yoke upon you and learn from Me, for I am gentle and lowly in heart, and you will find rest for your souls. For My yoke is easy and my burden is light."* A yoke is used to harness two animals together. In essence, being yoked together with our past, binds us to our past. In this passage, Jesus tells us to bind or remove ourselves from being bound to our past hurts and take His yoke upon us by binding ourselves to His love, His will and His way. We must be harnessed, yoked and bound together with Christ. We must replace the burdens of our hurt with His love.

My understanding of things was vague and full of cloudy days and misery. By telling me to stop, God revealed that I must do nothing more. He revealed that my laboring and trying to handle life on my own has been replaced. It was time to allow the Holy Spirit to dictate my every move. When I realized the scriptures said to meditate day and night, I began to do just that. I have learned to consult with Him about every decision. And no, I am not always obedient. This, too, is a process.

This world, as we all know, is FULL of lies and deceit. So, I am learning to do just the opposite of what I see many doing and not conform. Better yet, I am transforming my thoughts and bringing them under the subjection of the Will of God. He promised that He would give us the desires of our heart. And in my studying, I am learning that this task is much easier accomplished when my desires are lined up with His will for my life. Therefore, I seek to do God's will. Replace everything you think about your past and present situation with what God says. Then, decide to live again.

Queens Supporting Queens

Queen
1. The most powerful chess piece that each player has, able to move any numner of unobstructed squares in any direction along a rank, file, or diagonal on which it stands.
2. the female ruler of an independent state, especially one who inherits the position by birth.

Queens Supporting Queens

CHAPTER 4
Poetry for A Queen
La Tonya Day

    I have been pondering on what to write to you for quite a while now. I don't take this opportunity lightly because you are God's child. That would make you my Sister, whether I know you or not. In this writing I will give you everything straight from my heart. It's a collection of a few different things that I've experienced or learned along the way. I figured why hold on to it when it's something that I can say. I pray that you are blessed by this anthology written by different queens. I'm thankful because God wants His children working as a team. Philippians 2:2 tells us to be in full accord and of one mind. I'm sure in this compilation is what you will surely find.

    This life can be unpredictable, disheartening, and downright tough. I've thrown my hands up many, many times saying, "enough is enough!" The challenges in life can sometimes make us feel as if we are unable to go on. Well I'm here to tell you my sister, there's a reason why you were born!! Your life has such great purpose and so does your gut-wrenching pain. Yes, there will be beautiful sunshiny days along with some pouring down of rain. It's amazing how life can seem to turn quickly from good to the worst.

    In those moments I do my best to remember to go to God first. Although during those moments, I know that sometimes it can be a challenge for you to pray. Just know that our loving Daddy understands the tears and your dismay. Sometimes you will be lost for words and don't know exactly what to say. Our Father, with His outstretched arms will tell you it's going to be okay. My heart has been crushed, broken, and I've been betrayed. Believe me I feel you, I wanted vengeance to be paid.

    Anxiety and depression seem to be spreading like wildfire among the earth, but today I'm going to do my best to help you refocus your thoughts on your glorious rebirth. That doesn't mean that I am discounting anything that you may have gone through. I just want to help you to move forward and share some things that you can do.

    Cry out to God sis, He's waiting to hear your voice. Daddy loves to see His daughters making Him their first choice. Nothing and nobody will ever be able to do what He can. Not mom, not dad, not friends, or even a man. God should always and forever be first in your life. According to Matthew 6:33 this should not be a surprise. Your posture is important when you come before the Lord. Your mind, spirit, soul, and body should all be on One accord. Do your best to listen more and talk a whole lot less. This is when the Holy Spirit can communicate with you the best. When your spirit meets his Spirit there's not many words that need to be said. Then our thoughts line up with His thoughts, thank the Lord the flesh is dead. One way to show

reverence is falling before God on your knees. Bowing down before our King makes Him very, very pleased. Laying prostrate is another sign of humility and respect. I know I've done this many, many times, feeling as if my life had just been shipwrecked. I have cried out periodically to God, asking the question, why. Not realizing at the time, it was to help me and others to fly. The pain that you will experience in life is definitely not in vain. Remember what I said before, there will be
sunshine but also there will be rain. Don't forget that during Springtime the rain helps the flowers to bloom. Your gift will bring you before great men and it will undeniably make the room.

Go before the Lord, in prayer consistently throughout the day. This will help your thoughts and body to remain aligned with His way. In addition to this at your request, there's nothing wrong with seeing a therapist. It can be helpful to talk about what you're going through. A therapist can give you guidance on what you can do. Don't be ashamed, your mental health matters. It's necessary sometimes when you feel like your life has just shattered.
If God is for you then who can be against you?? The weapons will be formed but they will not succeed. Your Father has a plan for you, He is aware of your every need. Jehovah Nissi already knows the end from the beginning. If you look at Deuteronomy 20:4 you will see that you are always winning. Don't be fooled by the things that don't seem to be going right. Distractions will
try to get your attention so that you will lose your spiritual sight.

There will be many people that you meet in your life that seem to come and go. A select few of them will stay around, with time you will soon know. Don't ever take it personal, that's just how the cycle goes. We need certain people at different times to help us spiritually grow. Some friends are for a lifetime and some are for a season. God has allowed it all to happen that way for a particular time and reason. When you know God is in control it will give you unexplainable peace within. Remember He is your Father, your Comforter, and your Best friend. Never let the naysayers lead you down the road of defeat. Remember in Psalms 23:5, there's a table for you…. please take a seat!! Jehovah Jireh, your Provider, will always feed you well. He did it for our brothers Paul and Silas behind the prison cell.

The Word of God is nourishment, like pure gold to our spirit. That's why it is a necessity that our ear gates continuously hear it. Second Timothy mentions itching ears and people turning away from The Truth. Please don't let that also be your path, stay loyal like our sister Ruth! Ruth was the committed daughter-in-law that stayed with her mother-in-law Naomi. Sometimes we can be like her and experience times that we are feeling lonely. We can have a thousand "friends" and a million may follow but if you don't have a relationship with God your life can still feel hollow.
Don't be so impressed with numbers, and if you do let it be about the
One. The Father, The Holy Spirit, and the sacrificial life-giving Son. It is Jesus

that leads you through the door of becoming complete and whole. The Holy Spirit does the inner work, the transforming of your soul. All relationships are important, that's why God put us here together. Choosing to work as the Body of Christ makes things work out for the better. Jesus said, "people will know who you are if you have love for one another." Always make the time to reach out and pray for ALL your sisters and brothers.

I want you to know that you are not defined by your past. All of us have made mistakes and those won't be your last. We all have done things that we're not proud of and truly regret, but God gives us a second chance so don't you dare fret. Hold your head up high my sister, you are born again! Praise God, you are no longer a slave to your sin. There is nothing that you have ever done that is far beyond forgiving. Jesus died so now through Him you can truly begin living.

Make the decision to forgive yourself. Only you can do this, not anybody else. Release yourself from the mistakes of your past. It is up to you how long the blaming yourself will last. I used to have a challenging time letting go of what I knew. Then I had to remember that it is God that makes ALL…THINGS…. NEW and that includes you! Praise God that you are no longer a slave to sin. Our Father took care of that when Jesus body was broken. Some of the experiences that happened to you were seeds to help you grow. Now you can take those seeds and help someone else that you may know. I know some hurtful scars may have been left, but if used right they can push you to be your best. There's no greater feeling than helping someone walkthrough what you've been through. Ask the Holy Spirit for guidance on exactly what you can do. Once you forgive yourself it's time to forgive everyone else. For some this task may be difficult to do. Especially after all that you've gone through.

Remember that forgiveness isn't for the other person, but for you. Bitterness and resentment are not feelings you want to hold on to. Science has proven the negative effects it can have on the human brain. Do your best to forgive those that caused your heartache and pain. I've covered prayer, relationships, and the reason to forgive. I hope that this advice I've shared will help you to truly live. The emotions you are feeling are not being discounted because they are real. The prayer that I've prayed for you is that you will begin to completely heal. Poetry for a Queen that has had her share of ups and downs. It's time for you to hold your head up sis and straighten your royal crown. Be Blessed and Healed.

La Tonya Day

CHAPTER 5
The "No!" that Changed My Life
Chaundra Nicole Gore

Scratching my head when I got separation orders, letting me know that the 26th of August was going to be my last day as a United States Army Soldier. Months before this moment in time hit me like a ton of bricks, I had a personal conversation with God. The conversation went something like this, "God I want to make Sergeant Major of the Army and I know I can do it. Will I make it God? How long will it take me to accomplish this Lord? Father if it is your will let it be done, but please let me know if that is not the path you have for me."

Well, God immediately took me on an intentional journey to find my authentic-self two-years prior to this date even arriving and then a journey to become a *Lens of Faith* for the people He chose for me to impact. God is very intentional about his plan for our lives. Jeremiah 29:11 *says "I know the plans I have for you."* Allow me to take you through my walk.

I loved being a Soldier. I was passionate about teaching, training, and motivating service members and family members. All I really wanted was to become the top non-commissioned officer – Sergeant Major of the Army. When I made master sergeant, I said to myself "I will make it no matter what." But I didn't consult with God whole heartedly about that statement before I made. Little did I know, God's plan wasn't the same as my plan.

My children were suffering from a lack of my motherly presence while I was stationed away from them, but it was much needed because God was dealing with me. Many days and nights I cried out to God and asked him why my family wasn't here with me and he just kept giving me task to complete. The very first task was to enroll in the master's program for leadership. God said, "Look daughter. You are here on purpose and nothing else will distract you. Start your program and I will get you through it; I promise."
I did just as I was instructed. And the feeling I felt come over me was the Holy Spirit. I began to learn how to pray effectively, strategically, and fervently. Many nights I laid out before the Lord and cried and prayed. God started to speak to me throughout the days ahead.

I maintained a 4.0 throughout my entire master's program and didn't even think twice about it. Then God said, "Okay daughter. Now I need you to start a speaking platform." I said, "Really God? What is the name of this platform?" I didn't hear anything right away, but I thought to myself about the fact that I had already birthed *Lens of Faith Photography* and that's when I knew, it was going to be called *Lens of Faith Speaks*.

I began researching places to speak at and how I was going to speak, how long I was going to speak and everything I needed to be a great speaker. One day I was meditating, and I heard God say, "I didn't tell you to get on stage and this isn't about you". I immediately stopped what I was doing and sat still. God had just convicted me in my spirit, and I asked him, "God where am I supposed to speak?" He said, "start a show online and shine your light onto others." I immediately kicked into high gear and started a live Facebook podcast. I didn't know how to find people to interview so I was just searching, and I stumbled upon my sorority sister who was selling a new book entitled "The Birth of HIV." I purchased the book and read the entire book in one hour. It literally blew my mind. The very next thing I did was contact her to see if she would be willing to be the first person on my show. She agreed and she was excited about the upcoming interview.

After securing the first interview, I prayed and asked God who would be next. Little did I know that God would take me through these steps every week to find each person He wanted me to shine my light on. I eventually repeated these steps so many times, I had finally reached my one-year anniversary. To God be the glory! I was not getting paid to do these interviews and I received no monetary gain, but I did get followers. Interested people, women and men of God who saw what I was doing, and they rallied behind me in support.

God said if you are faithful over a small thing, I will make you ruler over many. That word has resonated in my mind night and day and so when I reached one-year airing the live FB podcast, God placed a Bishop in my life. I interviewed this Bishop because I saw all the great things that he was doing with his radio show, I wanted to spotlight him, and I did. Little did I know it was a divine interaction, this Bishop paved the way for me to be on the radio with my own radio show- "Encourage Yourself". I was super excited, and I couldn't believe what God had done. I wasn't even thinking about radio at all; it came to me.

I have always remembered the scripture Proverbs 18:16 (KJV), "A man's gift will make room for him." This was really coming to light for me and I was so humbled and grateful for the opportunity. God opened a door I never even knew was possible for Him to open, but I learned to have faith. I didn't just get faith, but radical faith. The faith of a mustard seed faith. The kind of faith that makes people think you are crazy.

No one could really understand what was happening to me, but I knew God was the captain of my ship and the driver of my car. I learned to lean all the way on God for everything. My health started to deteriorate, physically and mentally I started to feel overwhelmed. My 19-year decorated career began to fall apart, one thing after the next started happening. My husband started cheating on me and my marriage started to fall apart very quickly, but in the midst of it all, God told me to keep focusing on Him. No matter what was falling apart around me. He told me he would show me, who was for me and who was against me. I kept praying, meditating, and discovering my God given purpose as motivational and inspirational speaker. I took a deep dive into the Bible and read it from front to back. Then God began removing gossipers, bad friends, manipulators, and critics from my life one by one. I didn't know what was happening, I couldn't really understand it, but finally I realized I was standing ALONE!

God strategically removed people from my life like a chess game. The good and the bad was working out for my good, that's exactly what the scripture says, Romans 8:28 (KJV). I know for sure that as things started to fall apart in my life, God was strategically building a NEW ME. I discovered myself by going to God humbly, surrendering everything that was burdening me and asking God for forgive me of my sins. These very steps removed the mask that I had placed on my life called – (Soldier for Life). God said, "Daughter, you are no longer a Soldier in the U.S. Army, but you are my Soldier in the Army of the Lord. I have been waiting on you to come to me, so I can use you for my glory." I knew at that point in time that God was in control of my life and everything was going to be all right.

My new relationship with God, was one I had been running from my entire life. I never knew how much of a friend I had in Jesus until I spent intentional time with him, day and night. God started to show me my flaws and my attributes. Here is where I learned to be "authentically me" and I didn't have to be anyone but me. I developed the *"Discovering you"* program and I was the first person to take the course. Here is where I did intentional work on ME. I spent days, weeks, and months learning who I really was and what I was really great at. God used the Army as a training ground for me to be tried, tested, and chosen to do his work for more people. Had I not gone through the trials and tribulations coming out the military, I would not have passed my test to be used by God on a bigger scale.

God uses anybody, broken vessels and all to show his POWER and Glory on our lives. God was the only person that allowed me to stand straight up, look myself in the mirror and affirm my day, although I made millions of mistakes and chose the wrong path on several occasions. Those were stepping-stones for me to learn from in order to impact someone else's life.

The very things we try to hold on to, are the very things that God wants us to let go so they he can step in and bless us. We have to learn to be okay with God's NO and his YES. He wants us to trust him when we can't track, trail, or see him. He wants to be our Father of all fathers, Doctor of all doctors, and Lawyer of all lawyers. He is the way, truth, and the life. The only way for us to see that is to WALK by FAITH and not by SIGHT. This takes radical faith. The type of faith that makes people think you are crazy. People think I am crazy because I don't' worry. I don't make myself sick thinking and crying and being angry. I had to learn how to let those things go and it was hard. Yes, there was a process, but I did it and I'm glad I did. It didn't matter that my husband turned his back on me for another woman. It didn't matter that I faced court martial and discrimination, it didn't matter that I lost my job, it didn't matter that my husband abandoned every bill at our marital home, and it didn't matter that I didn't have any income for 60 days. Why? Because all things worked together for my good! God was trying to see what I was going to do with nothing, and I passed the ultimate test of time. I leaned on God whole heartedly, through the pain, through the crying, and through the shame. You see, what the devil meant for bad, God will turn it around for your good, according to Job 1:12 (KJV).

Life teaches us as we live, but it is up to us to learn the lesson and keep moving. Everything in your life happens for a reason, you may not be able to understand it, but what I know for sure is that God told me "No" to being a soldier for life and elevated me to being a soldier for him full-time with no expiration date.

God gives us small things to see how faithful we will be, in order to elevate us to where he wants u to be. So many people prayed for my personal downfall, but God is always up to something greater. I walked by faith and not by sight for the first time in my life and guess what? God's word did not return void. What He said, He meant every bit of it and I will continue to stand on God's word.

I want you to understand that making God the head of your life is very rewarding. I'm not telling you something I don't know about. I am telling you about something I am living every day. When I decided to choose God, I lost many people, I stood alone, but I gained a better understanding of life and how GOD wants me to move. This has been a hardworking journey, so don't think it's without work, but the work you put in, is definitely a reflection of what God will give you in your life. Stop waiting on God, because God is waiting on you to WALK by FAITH and trust him whole heartedly, so that He can do what he does and give you your hearts desires.

The scripture faith without works is dead, is real. You have to do your part and put the work in. Trust me- it is a lot more than you think. Praying, fasting, reading the Word of God, attending church or getting in the company of like-minded people, and speaking the Word of God in times of trouble and times of cheer. Developing your own personal relationship with God is very beneficial to you being fruitful and multiply in God's will for your life.

Trusting someone you can't see is hard and that's where the faith of a mustard seed is needed. Think about this: do you trust the person you are in a relationship with? Have they ever failed you? Did you trust them again, why? Did you ever have to make a decision and didn't know how it would be accomplished? These people you have contact with on Earth have failed you, so why not try God, even if you can't see Him working?

Remember that God loves you unconditionally, while the earthly people may place a million conditions on why they may love you or not. Try God. He has never failed me yet.

CHAPTER 6
Honoring A Queen
Vanessa Scott

I am sitting here, in the quiet of the skilled nursing facility that my Mother has been in for the last 11 days. Before that, we were in the hospital off and on for a whole month. The hospital and the skilled-nursing facility have become my home. It is very rare that I leave her. I think this is just what God knew that I needed. The quiet time; just to learn how to lean and depend on Him.

I have had to watch and endure my Mother go through so much and not be able to do anything. I have always been the one that was in control. I was the one that everyone came to and depended on. As a child, I was really an adult. This season of relinquishing complete control is very humbling. This is my Mother's second bout with breast cancer. Her first diagnosis was in 1997 and then it returned in 2018. She went through the process of receiving a double mastectomy last year. But now the cancer has metastasized to her brain. Mom's seizures have been unrelenting. They have affected her speech, memory, her ability to walk and much more.

To know my mom is *definitely* to love her. She has always been a strong, quiet woman that allows her work to speak for her. She raised four children as a single parent and has always provided for us. It amazes me that even though my Mother hasn't been able to speak much, the hospital and skilled nursing staff felt her spirit. Everyone loves her!! She has favor with all the doctors, nurses, and nurse aides. It was so amazing to see that she was still having an effect on people. This blesses me because it goes to show her character, integrity and her spirit.

There have been days that were so difficult to watch her endure so much that I just broke down. I questioned if I was strong enough. I thought about what I would do if she didn't make it. I thought about how I would take care of her and many other things. All I could see was the reality of what was at the present moment. It consumes me at times.

I soon realized that I was under attack for my gift and purpose that God had on my life. I knew that this was a distraction, but I also knew that this is where my relationship would go to another level with God. He will get our attention one way or another. The object is to not resist what we are going through but see what lesson God wants us to learn.

There are some very specific times when God will get our attention. Those are during pain and suffering. You know that no matter what friends you have, no one can fill the void or stop the pain but an encounter with God. During death, the only person that you can call on in the midnight hour is God. When you experience a miracle, you know that God is the only One that could have done it. During times of trouble, when you think there is no way that it will work out, God has already worked it out. He will get the glory in all of these situations and show you just how strong and mighty He is. This is where your faith is stretched and increased. When you have quiet, alone time with God. He has your attention and now you are eager to hear from Him.

My faith is definitely increasing. I am now aware that trials, pain, loss, hardships and disappointments all come to make me stronger. It doesn't feel good when you are going through it. But know that it is necessary. We have to have our trials and tests to be able to share with others the goodness of God and also be here in the earth realm to show someone else that they can make it through. Sometimes God makes sure we are ready before we can go to the next level of blessings that God has for us. If we don't pass the test, we will definitely repeat the lesson until we do. I have had to learn this the hard way a lot of times. I am thankful to know that the situations are building character in me rather than giving the enemy any credit. He does try to distract but, in those times, we have to be even more steadfast in our praise, prayer and our worship.

Watching my mom endure so much is hurtful as well as encouraging. She is a fighter and it helps me to stay strong like her. She never allowed any obstacles to stand in her way. I try my best to do the same.

My momma fought a good fight, but God said it was time for her to take her much deserved rest. I am confident in myself as the woman she raised to continue her legacy of spreading love, being resilient, loving God and family. I have had an extraordinary role model that has made such an impact in my life. I was honored to take care of my Momma.

In Memory of Queen Christine Scott

2 Corinthians 5:8
"We are confident, I say, and willing rather to be absent from the body, and to be present with the Lord."

CHAPTER 7
My Survival Guide #1
The Big "C" is Christ
Queen Glenda King

Life is Priceless. Treasure your life. When life has a way of presenting trials you never foreseen, face them and overcome. Your survival is about being able to endure fiery trials, growing in maturity and coming through as pure gold. There is a society of people who need to hear your story of God's amazing glory! Share your testimony of the Good News!

When All Hell Breaks Loose, Break Loose on Hell! What do you do when all of hell is coming against you? I can only speak for myself and my personal experience in one of the greatest trials I have ever had to experience in my life. In Sickness and In Health! In December 2014, I married my second husband. I had not been married in 19 years. I had been proposed to within those years, but never married. We lived in our home in Maryland.

In August 2015, eight months after being married, I was diagnosed with an illness. I was truly surprised and didn't quite know what to think. I told the Lord, "Lord this is not my portion." I had thoughts like, "Why and why now?" I had just gotten married after waiting 19 years and have a husband to take care of, along with my blended family. I knew in my heart I wasn't cursed, and God didn't make me sick. I was being tried in the fire.

I decided I wasn't going to tell a soul, because, I didn't want my faith to hear any negative words. I was going to believe God to beat this illness. I didn't want to worry my family. I needed to believe God for myself without any distractions. I was informed by my physician and nurse, due to the nature of treatment I would be receiving, I had to tell my family. I needed chemo for a few weeks and a combination of radiation for a total of 4-6 weeks of treatment. I did not have any idea of what the effects would be to my health. I kept believing for my healing amid the report, but there was no change.

One day, something happened. I received a call from my family, that my youngest adult daughter was at work, had to be rushed to the hospital and please come. When I arrived, she was being well taken care of, but she had been there for a few hours. I asked everyone, why didn't they call me sooner? I was upset. They said, "Ma, she had gotten sick at work and we know how you act. You would have been too concerned, asking a whole lot of detailed questions, etc." I said, "You really think I would do that?" In my mind I thought to myself, I am a very patient person, but when it comes to my children, I need to be notified promptly. I jokingly told them to wait until they have their own children.

At that moment, I realized this experience was letting me know, you can't keep your diagnosis from your family and do it alone. It's not fair to them and to trust God. To God's glory, my daughter was treated and released. I had to obey the Lord. I let my husband and rest of the family know. We prayed and we were believing God for the best. My husband had already found a job and moved to Florida the previous month. Unfortunately, I could not leave Maryland and come to Florida for treatment. My doctors did not like the idea of waiting for insurance and getting treatment somewhere else. So, the pressure of us being together was a lot. I just could not get there.

Prayer Works! I am forever grateful to God, the Lord Jesus Christ and Holy Spirit, for my husband, family, friends, pastors, church family, co-workers, associates, medical teams, housekeeping, and even a few social media friends who prayed for my healing. We must never forget the goodness in the heart of men and women who take time to pray and take time to pray for you. I love you!

The Port. When treated with chemo, a port is surgically installed just below your shoulder area into your chest. This is where the medicine is injected. While waiting in the operating room to fall asleep so the surgeon could install my port, the enemy tried to fill my mind with everything opposite of God's word. He said, "Look at you. You are all alone and you're going to die!" Looking in the natural sense, I was alone in a cold room. A tear fell. I remember saying, "God are you real?" I quickly remembered the enemy is a deceiver. We must speak the Word of God! The enemy wanted me to question my beliefs and doubt God. I began to look in the spirit. I was not alone. I began to speak Hebrew 13:5... the Lord said he will never leave me or forsake me! Eventually, I dozed off from the sleep injection. I awakened and my port was in.

Chemo and Radiation. My youngest daughter drove me to Washington, DC to get a final test to confirm my diagnosis before treatment. My children took me to my appointments until my husband was able to get back to Maryland. I started with chemo and then radiation. My nailbeds were turning black and my face was changing. My hair was thinning a little. It was a very difficult time in my marriage, but we managed through it. I thank God for my husband and family's love, prayers and strength!

Caregivers Go Through A Lot, Too. They can feel helpless. They may feel anger and frustration because as some say, "I didn't sign up for this!" Then there are those who have kindness, patience and care. Praying and communicating through these times is the best course of action. This can strengthen and help with the healing process.

The Generals in the Faith. The Generals in the Faith helped me. I would listen to music with healing scriptures throughout the day. I would pray, read my word, praise and worship. I enjoyed listening to musical artists like

William McDowell, Elevation Worship and Mandisa. I'd listen to Pastor John Hagee read healing scriptures with music throughout the day. I would read my Bible. I read Joel Osteen's Mom, Dodie Osteen's book on her healing from cancer. Her faith was magnificent!

As I was going through my initial battle with my illness, Pastor Rod Parsley, Valor Christian College and Breakthrough Ministries, Columbus, OH and Pastor Mike Freeman, Spirit of Faith Christian Center, Temple Hills, MD were just coming out of their health battle. I would listen to Pastor Mike's wife, Pastor DeeDee Freeman, conduct warfare against the enemy for her husband's healing. This woman had strong and powerful faith. Then, I was encouraged by Pastor Rod Parsley giving his testimony of how God brought him through the vocal cord cancer radiation treatment. I prayed and believed if the Lord could do it for them, he could do it for me.

The enemy will take his time to try to break you down with accusations of reasons you are ill. He reminded me of my past, present and future. You must have the Word of God in you to truly fight the enemy! Your mind must be strong and determined. Keep building on your faith with hope and assurance that God is God! You can't focus on who died from your illness. Your story is not their story.

Near Death's Door. No Weapon Formed Against Me! About the third or fourth week into the chemo and beginning of radiation, I was becoming very, very ill. On December 31st of 2015, I was in great pain and admitted to the hospital. I was like Lord, Lord help me. If you have not personally gone through cancer and treatment, you don't know exactly how it feels. I was admitted into the hospital and remained there for three weeks or so. This stuff was kicking my tail. I made my personal war room video declaring and decreeing I am coming out of this! I made that video to remind me that I will have a testimony later. My body was so very, very weak and in great pain. I didn't eat well at all and I was getting smaller. The doctor said that if I had not had the weight I had in the beginning of this process, I probably would not have withstood the treatment. I think the doctor was a little fearful trying to get me to eat.

Life and Death is in the Power of Your Tongue. One morning, I received a call from my unit commander. I was weak, in pain and did not believe I had the strength to continue. God knew I needed to pull strength out of me. The words the commander spoke and concern that came through helped me to fight and live! He spoke to me like a Soldier! At the time, I was not only a Department of Defense Civilian, I was 2xs the Citizen, an E-8 Master Sergeant in the United States Army Reserve. I had found a unit in West Palm Beach, Florida. I am trained for battle.

But the most important armor I had to put on was my spiritual armor as found in Ephesians 6:10-12, *"Finally, be strong in the Lord and in his mighty power. Put on the full armor of God, so that you can take your stand against the devil's schemes. For our struggle is not against flesh and blood, but against the rulers, against the authorities, against the powers of this dark world and against the spiritual forces of evil in the heavenly realms."*

I remember my pastor coming in and my doctor wanted me to get another treatment of radiation, I just couldn't do it anymore. My Pastor began to pray. She said, "Enough is ENOUGH!" This ends today! No more treatments." Not a minute passed after her praying with me, and my doctor and his student assistant came in the room and said, I believe I've done enough, and you won't need any more radiation treatments. I looked at my Pastor and we were both elated! She said to keep saying each day, "You're getting stronger!"

Remember, life is priceless to be treasured and respected. Love what God loves and hate what God hates. Cherish each day you live and always forgive those who don't mean you well. Love everyone, especially the unlovable ones. Somehow, they were dropped along the journey of life; mishandled. Read, pray, praise and worship! Laugh those laughs that make you hold your stomach and bring tears to your eyes.

Revelations 3:11 says, *"Let no man take your Crown!"* I was able to survive because Jesus Christ died to save me, in addition to the many prayers sent out on my behalf. I still have purpose. I am called to bring the good news, outreach and to win souls for His Kingdom. For those Believers who went through the illness trial and are absent from their body, I believe they are present with the Lord and win a Victory Crown. I am Queen Glenda, Daughter of the Most-High King!

CHAPTER 8
Blessed Extractions
Evangelist Jackie Stamps

So, you were looking for life to be great. Things didn't work out the way you thought they should. There was something inside of you that you thought was perfect. But trouble just kept coming your way. No matter how hard you tried, it seemed like trouble was on every leaning side. You had gotten saved, and you knew who God was. Yet you were still struggling. You are always there to help everyone. But it just seemed like no one else was there to help you in your time of need. It seems as if the nicer you were, the more people walked away. You suffered losing friends, and no one else seemed to fit the mold. You kept trying to figure out where you fit in. You kept praying about it, but no matter what, it just didn't come together. You may have asked, "Lord, what am I doing wrong? Why is everyone walking away from me?" But there was something that God was doing inside of you.

In the word of God, he tells us, that He will never leave us nor will He forsake us. There was something that God was doing on the inside of you, but for Him to do this, He had to remove some unnecessary pieces of the puzzle. What are these pieces called? They are called "Blessed Extractions." I know you are wondering why I would call it a "Blessed Extraction." Well, just hang tight and we will get to that in a few minutes.

There are some things that God does not want in your life. There are some places that God does not want you to go. There are some people that God does not want to be a part of your destiny. God is changing you into a new person. God is creating a new image of him inside of you. But, for him to do a new work on the inside there must be some extractions. If you look back to when you had your first, second, or maybe 3rd dentist appointment, the dentist would take the time to look and see if there were any bad places on the inside of your mouth surrounding the teeth. Sometimes you may have cavities, broken places, or even loose teeth. Sometimes the best way that the dentist knows to fix those bad places, is to extract those teeth from your mouth.

Now when you think of the extractions that the dentist makes when he removes the cavities, the teeth, or whatever that he is working on he uses different measurements. He uses different tools to complete these extractions. He must use needles to give you a shot in your mouth to numb those places, so it won't be as painful when these extractions happen. But even with the injections in your mouth, and with all these tools, the dentist still makes sure that he makes the necessary changes for you to feel better.

In other words, the dentist is doing the work he has to do to make sure that your mouth will work effectively to do what it's supposed to do. There are some things, in our lives, that God must use. Tools that God may use may not come or feel like what we think they should feel like. The tools that God may use might cause scraping, pain, purging, and possibly cause you to be uncomfortable.

God knows the places that don't fit like they're supposed to. God knows what goes in you and He knows was necessary for you to keep. When God causes you to go through different extractions, you are not going to always like the way it feels. When getting an extraction there is a great deal of pain, and there may be a lot of pressure. But God will let you see that after you have gone through it for a little while, then there is healing. There are also blessings. We must go through some hurt and pain; just like at the dentist's office. Don't you feel much better after you've had that tooth extracted?

It takes a couple of weeks for it to heal. In other words, it takes time for it to get back to where it is supposed to be. Just like a tooth with a cavity, or a broken tooth, God uses tools, removing unnecessary people, moving you from a job that is not necessary to your destiny or even removing you from a marriage that wasn't necessary to your destiny.

You are going to go through some pain. But as you've heard people say before; there was a blessing on the other side of through. A scripture reads, *"Weeping may endure for night, but joy is coming in the morning light."*

We find out just like the pressure from a tooth being pulled, there are pressures in life. But we grow from the pressure through Jesus Christ. He also experienced pressure. God made the ultimate sacrifice when He gave his only begotten son. I found out that it was necessary for me to be separated from things that were not godly, to find out who I really was. What is my true true worth in God? Extractions may be painful, but they will make you better. But through the pressure and through the pain remember that scripture tells us, *"The name of the Lord is a strong tower; the righteous run into it and are safe."* Proverbs, 18:10.

If you are like me, some or all part of your story are very messy, but we must allow God to extract the bad things so the good things can be seen and brought out for the glory of God. Once God extracts those bad things, then you can truly see the worth of who God has truly created you to be. Always remember this, *"But you are a chosen race a Royal priesthood a holy nation a people for his own possession that you may proclaim the excellencies of Him who called you out of darkness into His marvelous light."* 1 Peter 2:9. You are Godly Women of Strength. So just remember that you can make it through it all. At the end you will welcome "Blessed Extractions."

CHAPTER 9
Unless He Be Drawn
Shagaina Clark

Baptized at a Primitive Baptist church at the age of ten years old, I didn't understand the meaning of being baptized. I just knew that the pastor gave an invitation and I accepted, along with a friend and a cousin. I always loved going to church and hearing the word, especially since it was my escape to get away from my crazy dysfunctional home life. I saw a lot of things as a child, and I endured a lot of pain. My Father was an alcoholic and my mother loved him. Because of the violence and dysfunction in their relationship, I decided in my mind that I wouldn't allow a man or anyone to control or abuse me.

My Mother and I didn't have that Mother-Daughter relationship that many people brag about. I suffered along with her because she hadn't healed and was holding a lot of hurt inside. My dad caused me to have a distorted view of men. I accepted the love he gave from a distance. When I saw him, I was happy and when I didn't, I didn't really think about it. I just thought that's how it was supposed to be. During the times of violence, I stayed with my Aunt or my Grandmother. I recall my mom shooting my dad. I guess she got tired of the abuse. This is the type of influence that eventually shaped my mind and heart to become numb to the world.

At the age of fourteen, I witnessed my first murder. A lady shot her husband while he was working on someone's car. I was on the news giving an account of what I witnessed. At seventeen, I was on the witness stand for the murder of one of my very close friends and a lady who were killed at the same time. At age eighteen, I spoke with my brother approximately thirty minutes before he was killed on my mother's birthday; at her birthday party.

There were many days and nights that I cried myself to sleep because I longed for peace of mind, love, as well as healing. I would write prayers on paper, some of which l I still have in a folder. I always believed in God. I loved to hear His word and I have always loved being around His people. It just seemed like everything wrong was always happening in my life.

The saying, "hurt people, hurt people", is so very true. A hurt person doesn't realize the effect of the hurt they inflict on someone, until it is too late. The prisons are filled with hurt people, hospitals and cemeteries are filled with hurt people. Even churches are filled with hurt people. I was tired of hurting and I used different measures to escape that hurt. My first escape was men. It didn't matter if they loved me or not, I loved the attention. I was very promiscuous and didn't see anything wrong with what I was doing.

I didn't realize it then, but now looking back I all I can do is shake my head. I became pregnant at nineteen years old. I didn't know who the father was. I wasn't really worried about taking care of my child, I was more worried about loving her the right way and being a good mother mentally, emotionally, and spiritually. I worked hard and I went to school. My stepdad was my backbone during this time.

My mom and I still didn't have a good relationship, but I ended up moving closer to her after I graduated school. During this time, I became involved with drugs. It numbed me more to the pain I was always feeling, and it filled a temporary void that I always felt in my life. I didn't have money all the time to purchase drugs and most of the time I went to places where I knew I could get drugs for free and other times I would trade weed for it because I really didn't like marijuana. I would have people come over to my house, and we would get high while sitting in the dark listening to music.

Eventually, I got pregnant with my second child. I remember getting high more and drinking more because I just didn't want another child. I can remember one time getting high early Saturday all the way until Sunday morning. A couple of people were still there with me. I had gotten tired and decided to go in my room. As I walked in the room, I saw my bible on the dresser. I don't know why in the world I wanted to read the Bible, but I opened it. It read, "Behold, I come quickly, and my reward is with me, to give every man according as his work shall be!"

When I tell you I was scared, I WAS SCARED! I went into the kitchen where the others were getting high, I still had the Bible opened to the scripture. They were looking at me like I was crazy! I *was* crazy, and they were about to be crazy with me. I told them to read it. The guy that was there said, "Man you are tripping, you are high!" The guy was right, but I didn't want to be high anymore. I went to my room and put on my clothes. I left and went to get my daughter from my stepdad's house. I didn't know where to go. Out of all places in the world to go, I ended up going to my mother's house.

Coincidentally, she was getting ready to see my nephew be baptized at the early service. I cried all the way there. After his baptism, I still felt the need to go to church. I rode around the projects and saw a girl from around town and we talked. She told me that one of the guys I used to buy drugs from was getting baptized! I knew I didn't want to miss it. Still high, still crying, and still not really understanding what was going on with me, I went to the church. I couldn't bring myself to go inside the sanctuary, so I stayed in one of the rooms in the back. Just so happened, the room across from where I was, is where my former drug dealer was being prepared for baptism. He came out of the room and I broke down even more! The tears would not stop flowing! It was the most beautiful thing to witness and I was so happy to see it for myself.

The rest of the day, I laid in bed crying on and off. One of my cousins called because she heard about me getting high, she told me I needed to leave the drugs alone. I knew I needed to, but I didn't know how. I slowed down getting high, but I didn't stop. It wasn't until this particular night, that I was keeping a relative's house. My personal drug of choice was always powder cocaine. This night I ran out of powder. All the dealers were out of town, or not answering the telephones. All I had in my possession was crack rock or what we called "reddy rocks." I remembered my heart beating fast. I was nervous at the thought of trying it. I wanted my high to continue, but I didn't want to try crack.

I took out a cigarette and crushed the crack down into it. I didn't know if I was doing it right or not. I didn't want the smell to linger in my relative's house, so I stood in the back door. I was between the door and outside, enough to blow the smoke out. I was trying to be very careful because I didn't want anyone to see me and it was raining hard that night. I struck the lighter to light the cigarette that was in my mouth. As soon as I did, the drops of rain soaked my flame and my cigarette. I threw the cigarette out in the yard and slammed the door. I ran into the room where I usually sleep if I spend the night. I cried out so loud to God as if He couldn't hear me. I cried, prayed and begged God to help me. If someone was outside, I'm sure they heard every word. I didn't care who heard me, I needed and wanted help!

When I stopped crying, I overheard a woman on television praying. She said that there was a woman crying out to God. I was the woman, and at that moment I knew that God heard me. I made up my mind that I was done. I wanted to live right before God, so I started going back to church. I attended the Church of God. I moved out of the projects to the other side of town.

Away from the influence of my past. All I had was God and my children. In October 2004, the past paid me a visit. I reconnected with a guy I used to date three years prior. He was running from his own demons and I guess I felt like the savior. I was trying to get him back to God and little did I know, he was helping me. One particular night we were on the phone reading through Isaiah. I began to notice that I understood what I was reading! After some time passed, he told me that he was going to get off the phone because he felt that God was drawing me. We eventually got off the phone and I cried out, "Lord what is it? What do you want to say?"

The next verse of scripture I read was Acts 2:38, *"Then Peter said unto them, Repent and be baptized every one of you in the name of Jesus Christ for the remission of sins, and ye shall receive the gift of the Holy Ghost."* I understood! I knew it was God's presence and I knew it was Him speaking to me! His presence was so strong that I didn't even want to go to sleep. Afterwards I thought about it. I said, "Lord I've already been baptized, but if this is what you want me to do, I will be baptized again!"

The next day, I felt an urge to go to Wendy's. I didn't even like Wendy's, but I got up and went. I could still feel God's presence over me. After I ordered my food, I saw some people washing cars in the parking lot. So, I went down to where they were. The lady came to the car and asked what she could do for me today. She handed me a brochure, I looked at it, and I was in shock. Written on the brochure was Acts 2:38! I told her immediately that wanted to be baptized! She and I rejoiced together! I was baptized the very next day and my life changed for the good. I just wanted to be right with God!

I am hearing His voice. I am still learning every day. God filled that void that was always present. It was Him that I needed all along. Not the men, or the drugs; not even my parents could fill the longing in my soul. Only He did what nothing and no one else could. I haven't done everything right and have strayed several times. What I know for certain is, God is Faithful! He is not a man that He should lie. When my mother and my father forsook me, the Lord took me in and still to this day He is teaching me His ways!

I know you're thinking about how many times I was baptized. Let me just say, the first times it was me establishing my own righteousness. The last time, it was God who drew me unto Himself! He Revealed Himself to me. He sought me out and He found me. He redeemed me, and He set me free!

CHAPTER 10
Accepting the Irreversible
Jackqueline Mondo - Apinyi

He was really confident with baby Loni's birth and he arrived the very night he was due for labor induction. He entered the world weighing just over 8 pounds. I recall October 27, 2007. The afternoon of his birth. It seemed like ages since they took my baby to the neonatal unit. Two days later as l sat by his unit in the ward, the surgeon spoke to me as l sat with him watching for life. Next to the ward at Evelina Children's Hospital London, I signed the consent of the surgery with the surgeon beside baby Loni and I. At that moment, I was relatively confident. I had faith it would go well. But I can't lie; I was scared, and it was painful.

Pain is pain and it has no favorites. It knows no race, no color, no age or religious status. I am not talking about physical pain but emotional pain. Emotional pain that comes from trauma. Generally, trauma is defined as "a psychological emotional response to an event or an experience that is deeply distressing or disturbing." Everyone processes a traumatic event differently because we all face them through the lens of prior experiences on our lives.

What makes it trauma is because we don't expect it and when it hits us, it is within the spirit and does not vanish with painkillers created by man. I must make it clear at this stage that no one chooses pain deliberately because if you knew the after-effects, no one of us would say those words- "you chose it and made a decision that would have consequences."

I mentioned earlier, pain chooses no one. The loss of anyone despite their age is painful, but the loss of a baby or young child is something no parent can ever be prepared for. Having lost a mother who fought for her health for years, I knew deep down inside God had somewhat prepared me for a loss that I would not be able to stand up with my head upright.

What I also know is that the pain of a mother is always a more emotionally excruciating one. It is the pain of she that God used to carry and nurture life. The loss of a newborn baby was what I never in life expected that I would face. This is the kind of pain I absolutely had or possibly have no words for but words that the Lord would have me share today. I believe this is my time to reach you; a mother or father who has experienced the loss of a child. If I do, my work is done. However, I want to say the Lord, has created his painkiller for this type of pain. Exodus 15:26 – *"I am the Lord who heals you."* This type of pain needs healing. God will not only heal but, He will cure, restore or make whole. He is faithful to restore our inner emotions.

I have searched within myself from the very first pain, trials and tribulations to the most recent that could be categorized in the above. I have come to say that I am still thankful for each of them. Although I cannot comprehend or understand some things, I have come to accept them as I took them to the feet of Jesus.

There is not much in my own power that I can possibly do to reverse the loss of a baby. Sadly, I have had to take the mockery to my healer Jesus. I held onto pain when I heard that the condition of my womb is equal to the condition of my baby. Let me add that, I also have two children with special needs. For this I say unto the Lord to help me accept what I can't reverse and pull me from the pit that makes one hide so deep in a dark place and shed tears till the heart almost gives up.

I was already a married mother to three lovely, healthy boys. What more was it that was going to be so painful it's unacceptable? I was joyfully involved in looking after them and how boisterous and joyful they were! They kept me busy.

About 7 years into marriage, I found myself looking out of the window over the Thames River in an empty postnatal room in Guy's Hospital London. It was a beautiful view of this part of London with all the beautiful night lights. Despite the exterior beauty, I felt singled out with the loss of a mother's joy of a newborn baby. My baby was not with me. I never knew I would be the one that pain would choose that night of October 30th, 2007.

I was still dealing with pain at all levels. I had just lost a mother that early February 2007. I travelled from the United Kingdom to Africa for her burial. I was still in bereavement mode. Secondly, I was dealing with my unborn baby's diagnosis of Patent Foramen Ovale, which is a congenital heart condition. After Loni's diagnosis at the five-month scan, we were given two Choices. The first choice was to terminate the pregnancy or second to give birth and have an open-heart surgery; not once, twice but three times during the first two years of his life. The words of the midwife rang through my mind. My mind and thoughts were in many places after that doctor's report.

The truth is, I had already carried my baby with faith after a five-month diagnosis and he was now here. A confident father, mother and surgeon gazed at him in the pediatric ward. The surgeon sat with me briefly and explained the process and gave a date for surgery. Much happens after a baby is born in a hospital during labor and delivery. My husband had missed the birth. He gave the explanation to the surgeon that we had three other children to care for.

Beautiful baby Loni was born on the 26th of October. I am not sure if it was God's plan to avoid the negative effects of induction and a post excessive bleeding. I bled continually after his birth. I did not even feel or know it until the numbers of midwives in the room increased and eventually included a senior obstetrician.

Then, I heard the midwife say, "Stay still, it's a matter of life and death". That's when I knew a spiritual fight had to start for my life as many lives were reliant upon me. Emotions were numerous and great deal of energy was being used for this. It could take a few moments, hours or even days to fight for my own life. My baby's life, his future, our future as a family, my other children was at stake. Was the trauma of a sick child not enough?

After a couple of childhood illnesses like measles, and an eye accident in childhood that almost left me blind, I now felt the spirit of death was chasing me. But I was more concerned about my baby at that moment. Because in this type of pain, the past does not matter. I had to deal with having a baby fighting for his life and he needed me to help him fight.

Early the morning of October 30th 2007, the phone rang at 6 am in the postnatal room. I was now in on my own. I was not with other mothers. After over eight hours in the surgery room, I was asked to go down to the pediatric ward. I hastily got ready and went to the ward. I took one look at the surgeon with his hands over his mouth gazing from one side, and my heart raced. The surgeon said the surgery itself went well but my beautiful baby Loni's heart kept stopping. Looking towards all the connections on his machine, I really had no words. The surgeon asked, "Is there anyone you would like us to call? Anxiety swept through me, worry swept through me.
I replied, "Yes, my husband".

This is the third time I was given painful news on my own. The first time was at his five-month scan when I was told to terminate the pregnancy, but we continued towards his birth and opted for surgery instead after he was born. Here we were! Is this why I carried him to birth? The thought raced through my mind.

Though we were told about the severity, we went ahead in faith. At this point I wanted God to show me that my faith in Him regarding my baby was not in vain. After all, they almost made me terminate my second son whom they, the sonographers, said had a high chance of having Down Syndrome. Thankfully, amniocentesis tests showed negative! Don't tell me these are emotions from the enemy because I had asked God to intervene. He was going to straighten crooked paths, right? Feelings of anger were setting in.

Nobody updated me all night and from the time baby Loni went to surgery the 2nd day after birth. The surgeon was confident of his outcome due to his healthy birth weight of eight pounds. The surgeon continued to watch from a distance. He sat down with his hands on his mouth like he had really missed it. He was watching from a distance as the doctors resuscitated the life into the tiny heart.

If ever there was a higher lack of empathy, it was then. The doctors looked like they had tried and were ready to call it quits. By that time my husband had arrived from home. One of the senior doctors called me a side and said, "Baby Loni lost his heart beat several times. They tried to resuscitate him several times within the two days after surgery, but his dear little heart began to stop fighting." The doctors thought it was now time to let him go peacefully. They did not know what his condition would be if he survived.

They said his condition may even include paralysis or possibly brain damaged, and this would subsequently affect his quality of life. Who would have boldness to say these things to a mother? Remember they were on duty. This is the point when I realized you never know another person's pain until you go through it. These doctors should have held me steady and taken my baby to a private room. But no, he was in the open and other worried parents were passing by. The demeanor of the doctors and receptionist towards me seemed so cold. I did not want to be in this cold world anymore.

I experienced an extreme lack of empathy while on the Evelina ward. The receptionist was oozing a lack of sensitivity in her demeanor. She tells the nurse caring for Baby Loni who had audacity to tell me to go rest and that I looked bad. I was a new mother to a baby who was going into a surgery with a heart condition, I almost lost my life and now I am dealing with postnatal emotions! I kept still. Peace be still in tumultuous emotions. I had no energy or inkling to handover my sanity to ignorant insensitive comments.

An unusual and unexpected type of anger was beginning to rise in my spirit. At this point, one might be asking where God was in all this. Did I not say in the beginning, I had faith in God and that I had taken everything to Jesus? Yes, I sound angry because these were the first few emotions mixed with pain and many more post birth. Hormones also had their own work going. My body now had to deal with a baby that was born but not there to feed milk that was building reserve in my maternal glands. We had a cot at home but no baby to bring. I had a body to show that I was post birth but no baby.

Baby Loni was laid to rest on the 30th of October 2007. It was just 4 days after birth. I say thank you Lord for enabling me to share how far you have brought me in overcoming the pain of loss and shame that accompanies anger and sorrow. I could not have done it without God. *"I am the Lord who heals you."* Exodus 15:26

You can heal through the most adverse level of pain through the power of the Holy Spirit whom you allow to dwell in you. Through worship and praise, over time it shall be so. To a mother in loss, you may not comprehend it but remember, Psalms 73:26 which says, *"My heart may fail, but God is the strength of my heart and portion forever."* It is not the physical heart per say but spiritual heart. I can only sense the pain of a mother who has lost a baby or older child. Having been through those very painful emotions. He shall strengthen you in your weakest moments. Eph. 3:16 says *"I pray that out of His glorious riches He may strengthen you with His power through his spirit in your inner being."*

Embrace Him with all your might. Ask him for comfort that only He can provide. It is your very faith that will help you through. When Mary's brother Lazarus died, Jesus heard and left Judea after two days. He had already started going through the emotions of pain. By the time he arrived, he was able to comfort Mary. Jesus was close to Lazarus and his sisters. He is close to the broken hearted. Martha ran out saying to Jesus, John 11:21 *"Lord if you were here my brother would not have died"* I remember questioning God during that time of loss. Admittedly I had lost faith as a young Christian trying to understand loss.

My mother had died earlier that year in February and I was still mourning her. I was close to my mother. I recall saying, she was not there to talk to about my pain and loss. I recall two ladies who prayed for me and said I should let go. The other prayed for my healing, saying that I will one day bring words of encouragement to a mother in pain from loss.

Those afflictions were many, but today the pain is healed. Psalms 34:19 says *"Many are the afflictions of the righteous but the Lord delivereth him from them from them all."* God has delivered me from the pain of my afflictions and released me into His peace of mind that surpasses all human understanding, according to Philippians 4:7.

Because I cannot reverse the physically irreversible loss but overcame it and here, I am released out of pain to testify of His goodness. A goodness that is available to you. He is knocking at your door ready to help you overcome it. It will take time, but it is worth it if you avail yourself.

On the 31st day of October 2019 at 6.30 a.m., the pain of loss swept through me like it was today. The tears revisited every fiber of my being and I said Lord, I thank you for releasing pain of the loss. It has been painful but thank you Holy Spirit for enabling me to not only accept but to overcome what I thought I never would because it turned out irreversible physically.
But you reversed it *emotionally*. By His grace and His stripes, you will be healed from emotional pain.

I thank God for my husband David Apinyi for standing up by me in the pain when I had numerous emotions and my children Jesse 21, Ocol 19, Bishop Luwum Janani 15 and Chan Apinyi 10. You could have had a brother who now sleeps in the Lord. He left too early, but he is not in pain.
We love you baby Loni. Continue to sleep in the Lord. I thank the Lord for using Evangelist Tanya Thompson of Glory after the Rain Ministries for allowing me to present a word of encouragement. It has been a blessing writing this and trust it will bless you.

Jackqueline Mondo-Apinyi
Woman Arise and Be Healed

CHAPTER 11
Unable to Breathe
Christy Adams

Have you ever suddenly had the breath knocked out of you without warning and found yourself unable to breathe? Maybe you were in a fight and got punched in the stomach before you even knew what was happening. Or maybe you jumped into a pool from the high dive, landed the wrong way in the water, and instantly found yourself struggling to get to the surface so that you could get air--only to find that once you had your head above the water, you still couldn't breathe.

What actually happens when you get the breath knocked out of you is called a diaphragm spasm. Our diaphragm is a large muscle that constricts when we breathe and helps us to pull air into our lungs. But when a diaphragm spasm takes place, the diaphragm is literally paralyzed for a minute. All of the air in your lungs is emptied out suddenly and your body feels intense pain for what seems like eternity but is only a few seconds. It's very scary at the time because you want to breathe but it's as if your body has forgotten how. You fight to draw air into your lungs, but you can't. The best thing you can do, however is relax and allow it to happen naturally. But at the time, when you are hurting, it can cause you to panic and fight for dear life to find a way to breathe.

I've been there and it's extremely scary and excruciating, to say the least; especially when a couple of people have to drag you out and lay you on the side of the pool so you can get your bearings. It feels like you'll never breathe again. It feels like your life is going to end and you'll die right there. But, eventually you do start to breathe through the pain.

Those events remind me of life and how when you least expect it, out of the blue, BAM! Something happens and the breath seems to be knocked out you. I don't mean in a literal sense, but when things take you by surprise, it can feel as though you can't breathe anymore, as if you're paralyzed. I'm sure that each of you can relate to what I'm describing as well.

It happened to me when my mom passed away unexpectedly on July 1st, 2005. She had gone in for a simple heart catherization at seven am that morning, but complications arose, and she was dead by six o'clock that evening. I was caught off guard by death's sucker punch and it felt as if the very breath left my body when I saw her purple lips and fingers.

I can't explain every feeling that flooded through me when I realized she was gone, but it was the most horrible thing I have ever lived through, to say the least. I was in sudden shock, much the same way when I landed on my back in the pool. It felt as if the pain knocked me off my feet and I couldn't get up. I literally could not draw air into my lungs for a few seconds when they told me she had passed away. It was devastating. I felt an ache in my chest that I'd never felt before. It was a literal ache, a physical pain that I did not realize could accompany sorrow. I had to try and calm down and tell myself to breathe. I had to wait a few minutes and try to relax because I felt as if I was going to die as well.

After I got over the initial shock of the news and finally was able to breathe again, I still wasn't okay. It took me a very long time to move past the pain. Don't misunderstand me; I will never get over it. There will always be a sadness there, a void, but the pain does subside somewhat over time. I was finally able to get my breath back after what felt like my body being paralyzed for a while.

I'm reminded of another example that a friend experienced many years ago that is somewhat different in that it doesn't involve death, but it was an event that left him with a sudden feeling of the breath being knocked from him, nonetheless. He had owned his own business for many years and was doing well financially. He trusted his accountant to take care of all things related to the business end of it, because she was, after all, the accountant.

On a hot July day while going about his business, working and living life, his wife opened a letter from the IRS. It stated that they owed many, many thousands of dollars in taxes that had to be paid immediately. His wife began reading what the letter said and after hearing the entirety, my friend grabbed his chest and collapsed onto the floor. He told his wife that he thought he was having a heart attack. The breath had been knocked out of him, in a sense, by the news he'd just received. It turned out his accountant wasn't on the up and up and she had taken advantage of him and several of her other clients, leaving them all in dire straits with the IRS, while she fled with the bulk their money.

My friend laid there on the floor, trying to figure out how to breathe again and how to fix the mess he had not made. He was essentially, paralyzed by the devastating news. After a while he was able to get up and carry on, eventually making a deal with the IRS to pay what he owed. And he was able to get his breath back after life had sent him that horrible blow for which he hadn't asked.

There are many ways that circumstances can knock the breath out of us. It may be a death, like in my case, or an instant financial crisis, like in my friend's case. You may have suddenly suffered the loss of a job that you needed to provide for your family, or you may have lost your home due to fire or being behind on payments and ended up having nowhere to go. All of those things can knock the breath from you, leaving you paralyzed on the floor. Each one can cause you to feel as if you'll never breathe again, as if your lungs will never take in the air you need to sustain your heart and life.

But you will, eventually. I know, because I have gone through EACH one of the things listed above. I've lost a job, a loved one, a home, as well as suffering the sudden financial crisis that left me stunned and not knowing what I was going to do to provide for my family or myself.

We are all the same and we all go through life's battles and trials. Life has a way of bringing pain to us all. The Word of God tells us in Job 14:1 *"Man that is born of a woman is of few days and full of trouble"* KJV. We know that to be true. It seems like each day when we wake up there is something else that will try and rob us of our joy and bring pain to our lives. But I want you to know that with the help of God, we can overcome anything that comes our way.

When my mom died, I was in a complete tailspin. She was a nurse and had been living with my grandfather (her dad) while he was dying of cancer. So, when she suddenly passed, that left my grandfather with only me to care for him. I knew nothing of what to do. I didn't even know what medicines to give him that were on the bathroom counter. It took me a couple of days to get it all lined out (with the help of his doctor) and then plan my mom's funeral. No sooner had we gotten her buried, then my grandfather died a few days later. That was one of the hardest times in my life. I had never experienced grief and sadness like I did when they both left us.

Our lives were never the same. There was an emptiness that will never be filled by another human. I began to grieve deeply for them both and in that grief, I allowed the sorrow to turn to depression. I was not paying attention to how deep I had slipped into the sadness and then before I knew it, I couldn't even function. It was a very dark time in my life. My husband at the time worried about me, my son worried about me, my friends and my sister all worried about me. But none of them knew how to help me. Even I didn't know how to help me.

I had stopped going anywhere. I stopped talking to people on the phone. I basically stopped living. But thank God for a friend from church who sent me a letter one day. She included in it 52 places in the Bible to read and she promised me that I would take the time to read them, that God would help me. So, I did. I sat down and read those verses every day. I found myself writing them down and reading them over and over until they were all ingrained in my spirit and hidden in my heart. Over the next year and a half, I clung to them as if they were the only line that I had between me dying or living. I can't express to you exactly how much those scriptures meant to me, but I can tell you that they got the breath back into my lungs and helped me live again.

"There is something powerful in the Word of God. It pierces even to the dividing asunder of soul and spirit and it's a discerner of the thoughts and the intents of the heart." Hebrews 4:12. It can heal and transform you when read it and it will light your path and give you direction.

There is healing to be found in His Word. No matter what you are going through, I know it's hard at the present time, but get a Bible and read the Scriptures. They will help you; I promise. There is something in there for every situation you face. There is a comfort to be found in the God's Word.

Although you don't feel like life will ever be the same again, and you feel that you won't ever breathe again, you will. It will take a while for you to draw the air back into your lungs, but it will come. Trust God to help you. He's the only One who can.

Helpful Verses:
*Hebrews 4:12; Proverbs 3:5; Revelation 21:4; Psalm 147:3; Psalm 73:26;
1 Corinthians 13:7; 2 Corinthians 5:7*

Queens Supporting Queens

CHAPTER 12
Look at Her: A Story of Forgiveness
Jamilah "Beautiful" Cooper

I look at her. I couldn't do that before, but now I can. I can look at her for a long time when she lets me. It always feels like watching an onion; waiting for it to peel its own layers back. I know it's not going to happen. I know that it would only make me cry if it did. I know she's mostly an onion, but sometimes she's not so closed off. Sometimes she completely transforms into something much more open. Not open intentionally, but open like an egg that's accidentally been knocked off the countertop. Not usefully broken like eggs that eventually become breakfast; but rather a shattered mess to clean up. But I can still look at her. I look at her for a long time and I wish she was neither an onion nor an egg. I wish she was just my Mother. After forty-one years as the daughter of a bipolar sufferer, I have to say this is still my wish.

Having a parent that suffers from severe mental illness is challenging on several levels. When I was small, I wanted to look up to her, trust her, and depend on her but I couldn't, and I didn't understand why. In adolescence, I initially wanted to understand her and help her. But after too often being a target for her to take out all her anger, aggression, fear, and mania on, I eventually just wanted to either hurt her back or escape her. But I never did really hurt her, and by the grace of God I did get the opportunity to escape. Her abandonment of me when I was thirteen was my deliverance; though it didn't feel that way at the time.

At the time, I felt like a balloon being let go by a child who didn't know she was supposed to be careful with it. And somehow, even then, I still wanted her. I was afraid and confused and so angry, but I still wanted - make that needed - my Mother, and I resented her for not needing me. It was a long time, several years in fact, before I could bring myself to even acknowledge her again after that.

It was a few more years before I was able to forgive, and forgive, and forgive again. Knowing that God commanded me to honor her and having to allow Him to show me where to even begin to do that. Harboring the fear of inheriting her illness in the back of my mind. Clinging to caution in her presence (or avoiding it all together) for the sake of both of our hearts. Forgiving, and forgiving, and forgiving again.

Finally, today, I can look at her. I can look at her and not mind if I see myself. Sometimes, I can even actually see *her*. In some very brief put precious moments, I can see quick glimpses of an altogether lovely woman that I never quite got to know. And I look for as long as she'll let me;

without speaking or moving or breathing… Futilely trying not to do anything that might disturb whatever atmospheric conditions have haphazardly set her in balance. A relative split-second of a warm, musical radiance. I can see her, and I can see where I came from. Such sights wouldn't be possible for me if it hadn't been for God opening my eyes to my mother through the power of FORGIVENESS; a tool He created to help free us from the bondage of grudges, resentment, anger, hatred, and the like.

With my mother's condition being what it is, God knew that the amount of connection I would be able to have with her wouldn't be much. For a very long time I questioned God's decision to bring me to life through her and into such a situation of shortage. I questioned the purpose of a creation like her. I couldn't see whatever God saw. Because of this, I've lived a lot of my life forfeiting those tiny, spiritually nutritional pieces of connectedness that I do get to have with her, all because I was angry and thought that distance was the best way to deal with it. Not realizing that those are God's answers to my many prayers to just "have my Mama."

The answer I was expecting when I prayed for my mother was for God to magically make her into *Claire Huxtable*. He of course did not do that, so I opted to keep my distance. But as it turns out, the more I distanced myself from her, the worse I felt. After a while that anger was terrible to hold on to, and it was making me physically and mentally unstable. It was making me like her in ways I never wanted to be.

At the same time, it was giving me some understanding of how her own bottled up issues from childhood may have led to her current mental state. That understanding made me more open to receive what God had to say about forgiveness. Because I truly did want to forgive her, and I wanted to be forgiven for my unforgiveness. The weight of it was becoming too much to bear, but I didn't know how to put it down. When I went to the Bible for help, I quickly noticed a frequent reiteration of the example Christ set for us and how He designed forgiveness to work:

> *Be kind and compassionate to one another,*
> *forgiving each other, just as in Christ God forgave you.*
> *- Ephesians 4:32*
> *For if you forgive other people when they sin against you,*
> *your heavenly Father will also forgive you.*
> *- Matthew 6:14*
> *Bear with each other and forgive one another*
> *if any of you has a grievance against someone.*
> *Forgive as the Lord forgave you.*
> *- Colossians 3:13*

> *Do not judge, and you will not be judged.*
> *Do not condemn, and you will not be condemned.*
> *Forgive, and you will be forgiven.*
> *- Luke 6:37*
> *And when you stand praying,*
> *if you hold anything against anyone, forgive them,*
> *so that your Father in heaven may forgive you your sins.*
> *- Mark 11:25*
> *Then Peter came to Jesus and asked,*
> *"Lord, how many times shall I forgive my brother or sister*
> *who sins against me? Up to seven times?"*
> *Jesus answered, "I tell you, not seven times,*
> *but seventy-seven times."*
> *- Matthew 18:21-22*

Over and over and over I was reminded of how God constantly forgives me and how my unwillingness to forgive others just kind of negates all the forgiveness I've received. In order to rectify this, I had to try following the Lord's example of continually forgiving. But not being ready to speak to her at the time, let alone fix my mouth to say the words "I forgive you."

I'll admit that it wasn't an easy thing to do in the least. I knew I couldn't possibly do it on my own, so I asked the Lord how in the world I was supposed to even begin this gut-wrenching process. That's when the Holy Spirit told me to simply... "Look at her."

And that's just what I did. Starting with just studying her pictures. Searching my memory for the good pieces of her. Listening to other people's stories and memories of her. Meeting her again, but at my own pace. A while later I advanced to having brief interactions with her.

These interactions often proved to be a flight too close to the sun, for which I'd end up having to forgive us both, but they were accomplishments, nonetheless.

Eventually I was able to find and form the words to tell her how I was feeling in much needed conversations... and some arguments, but mostly civil conversations. Forgiving again, every step of the way. And now, by the grace of God, she and I can share entire days together - be they pleasant or otherwise - and I give Jesus all the credit for that. And when she's being an onion, or an egg, I can just look at her. Watching for my Mama. Waiting to embrace her when she lets me. Resting in God's embrace when she doesn't. Exercising forgiveness day by day.

Being a Mother now myself, repairing my maternal relationship is more important than ever. The thought of having any one of my four children being estranged from me, for any reason or period of time, is absolutely devastating. And though I keep them very close to me to avoid having them experience the pain of separation, I'm aware that it's counterproductive and confusing for them to see me at odds with my own Mother.

So, for that reason, I'm making an even more determined effort and looking even closer into fixing what's broken with my Mother and me. Because I refuse to have any of that poisonous spirit of unforgiveness to continue for even one more generation.

Daily, I pray that God forgives me for every unkind word or ill thought I've ever directed toward the Mother He gave me. I thank Him for the moments of clarity in which I get to experience her in a motherly way. I trust his plan for making me her daughter. I draw from His strength when that gets to be too hard. And I forgive my Mother and myself as many times as necessary. It is a lot of work, but there's a freedom and a growth in this task that I didn't have when I allowed unforgiveness to keep us apart.

There's a bond developing that wasn't possible when we were enemies. We're still not as close as a Mother and daughter could ideally be, but I can honestly say that we are closer than we ever were. And all thanks to God and His gift of forgiveness… Look at us now.

Queens Supporting Queens

CHAPTER 13
Who Am I?
Kimberly Gore

Who am I? This question is such a loaded question for us women. Rarely do we know who we are, or even who we are purposed to become. Many things have made us come to this conclusion. We let the wiles of life define who we are. Disappointments, anger, abandonment, loneliness, fear, abuse and whatever else that seems to have us bound. We get so tied down that we see no other way. All around us is darkness and it appears to be no hope for today and surely no hope for tomorrow. It's like being stuck in a room with no way out. All we know to do is look around us. Which we only see the same four walls. Same size, color and texture. Never once do we look up to which cometh our help.

Look up to see something different. Look up to our Heavenly father that has been waiting all along for us to ask him to step in. You see, I know the feeling all too well. The feeling of being stuck with nowhere to go or no one to turn to. I was so numb inside from disappointment and not knowing who I was as a Woman of God. I was confused about my identity. And no this wasn't when I was a youth. I was a grown woman and still didn't have a clue. I just want to be open and honest with you.

After I realized who I was, my vision became clear and I could breathe again. God was there all along waiting on me to just look up.

Heaven is lined with angels rooting for us. Waiting on us to call out to our Heavenly Father to come and walk this thing called life with us. He won't bombard our lives so he's patiently waiting. Once he hears you cry out to Him, your life will never be the same.

We were created to walk upright, proudly but humble. Hold your head up sis. No more shame, guilt, insecurity or doubt. That is all the things of the past. Don't get me wrong, storms will continue to come your way, but the difference now is that, you know where your help comes from.

You are never alone. We are all in this together, holding each other up. No one is being left behind. That's why it's so important to lift each other up. Be a listening ear, smile at someone, give a hug or if you see someone looking confused or down and out, ask if they are okay and be willing to be there if they aren't.

We are connected by the stories of our past, present and future. Good or bad, our stories are what transform us into the Queens we are today. We are not the disappointments of our past. We are God's beloved. We are Royalty! In 1 Peter 2:9, But you *are* a chosen generation, a royal priesthood, a holy nation, His own special people, that you may proclaim the praises of

Him who called you out of darkness into His marvelous light. Nothing can change our birthright. Nothing. We have that signed and sealed and nothing can take that away.

The fact that God cares so deeply about the things that concern us, sends a radiant light all throughout my body. I know that someone loves me unconditionally. So, when people let us down, trust that God has your back. There is no doubt in my mind that my Abba Father smiles when he watches me trying to fulfill the purpose on my life. He calls me His own. I am His daughter. He is my father. If you think you are alone and have no one to call on, He's waiting. Waiting with open arms and a forgiving heart. He's waiting with a smile on his face. He's waiting on you!

My Dear Queen, today is a new day. All things are made new with God. You don't have to be perfect. Not one person is. We will make mistakes even while walking this journey and it's okay. Just keep striving until you get it right. Don't worry about judgement or the ones what gossip behind your back. Sooner or later they will have to walk this journey as well. Just pray for them and keep on moving.

Many times, throughout my life I can honestly say I was confused. I was looking for someone to fill the void I had within me. Maybe it was the lack of a true father in the home growing up or maybe I just wanted to follow my own rules. Whatever it may be, I found out that no one could fill the emptiness that I felt.

Everything seemed so temporary and I later found out that it was. I now know that nothing can take the place and give you a radiant peace like God can. I can't even fully express the change that I feel within my life. I sometimes catch myself just smiling. Smiling even in the midst of having an absence of what I would call life's essential things. I still smile because I know the promises, He has given me and everything I need is a testament to my faith. I know he does not make empty promises and only wants the best for me and guess what? He wants the best for you as well.

My life was consumed with raising my family and dating. I never had the time or interest to really find out who I was as a person. What are my likes and dislikes? What makes me happy or unhappy? What makes me really tick? So, in my 40's trying to learn myself, was somewhat a challenge. At this point, why does it even matter what makes Kimberly," Kimberly" right? Well wrong. God will restore the years the cankerworm stole. Joel 2:25 says, *"And I will restore to you the years that the locust hath eaten, the cankerworm, and the caterpillar, and the palmerworm, my great army which I sent among you. If he will do that for a worm, surely, he will do it for you and I."*

It's never too late to find your purpose, live out your dreams and set goals and fulfill them. If you are starting over today, then today is the first day of the rest of your life. Rejoice and be glad we have a heavenly father that never gives up on us. He knows our start from our ending.

"I make known the end from the beginning, from ancient times, what is still to come. I say, 'My purpose will stand, and I will do all that I please." says Isaiah 46:10. If the one that made us isn't giving up, then what gives us that choice. Keep pushing, keep striving, and keep going until you reach the best version of yourself. And, when you get there, don't stop because there is still so much more to be done.

After all, if we are breathing there is still more work to be done. We should be waking up every day with a heart full of gratitude, because he chose us to continue with his mission in this earth.

You don't have to have letters behind your name or some fancy title, just be ready and willing. I would always ask myself what makes me think I am qualified to write a book. I'm just plain ole Kim. A girl that grew up in North Nashville and was raised by a single mother, raised 3 children as a single mother and only recently went to college! So, in my eyes there is nothing special at all about me. BUT God says otherwise. He adores me and this I know. He has kept my family wrapped safely in his arms, time and time again. Even when I didn't know what to watch out for. God knew.

Be excited about your life and what's to come in your future. Somethings will cause sorrow, but joy will always come in the morning. Nothing that happens to us is by accident. It all has a purpose and a plan. Do we always understand? No. Do we often question why? Yes. Is it okay that we do this? Of course, it is. We don't have to always know the answers and its okay to ask, but just know everything isn't meant to be revealed. We just have to boldly walk in faith and keep trusting God.

In closing Queens, we are fearfully and wonderfully made in God's image. Every last one of us. God does not love us any more or any less, because of the way we look, where we come from, or because of mistakes that we have made. Remember He knows all. He wrote the book of our lives and has allowed time for all our detours and unexpected stops along the way. I may never meet you in person, but we are Sisters and Queens in the Kingdom and will forever be tied together in love.

Below are some scriptures that have kept me going on my journey.

Ephesians 3: 20-21
Now to him who is able to do immeasurably more than all we ask or imagine, according to his power that is within us, to him be glory in the church and in Christ Jesus throughout all generations, forever and ever! Amen

Psalm 1: 1-3
Blessed is the man who does not "walk" in the counsel of the wicked or "stand" in the way of sinners or sit in the seat of mockers. But his delight is in the law of the Lord, and on his law, he meditates day and night.

1 Corinthians 2: 9
However, it is written: No eye has seen, no ear has heard, no mind has conceived what God has prepared for those who love him."

Jeremiah 29: 11-12
For I know the plans I have for you, "declares the Lord, "plans to prosper you and not to harm you, plans to give you hope and a future. Then you will call upon me and come and pray to me, and I will listen to you.

Psalm 34: 8
Taste and see that the Lord id good; blessed is the man who takes refuge in him. Those who fear him lack nothing.

Amos 9: 13-15
Yes indeed, it won't be long now. God's Decree. Things are going to happen so fast your head will swim, one thing fast on the heels of the other. You won't be able to keep up. Everything will be happening at once and everywhere you look, blessings! Blessings like wine pouring off the mountains and hills. I'll make everything right again for my people **Israel.**

CHAPTER 14
Knowing Who You Are
Janice Blackmon

While the chatter of voices could be heard throughout the gymnasium the screams and shrills of children laughing and playing echoed throughout the Bryant Junior High School gymnasium. My PE teacher struggled to regain control over a large group of children waiting for the weekly kickball game. It was 3rd period.

Each Thursday of each week was a day in particular that the closer it got, the more I dreaded it. Those were the days of my youth, days when I was made to feel as if I wasn't fast enough, smart enough, strong enough or good enough.

As the teacher began to call out the names of the team captains (the title that I knew that I would never need to worry about being chosen for) , there I stood in the back, as I normally did , with a group of children who were eager and who were anxiously awaiting to be the next to be called on to be placed on the team. To be among the ones who were chosen to be on the winning team was such an honor!!! As the choices became smaller and smaller, the names continued to be called, and the sizes of the group dwindled down to those being chosen last. The rejects.

I was never really into sports, and so being chosen to be on the kickball team with a group of my peers frightened me beyond words!!! Why couldn't they just call the ones that had a desire to play? I don't know what the problem was, after all Kickball was something that we all would play within our neighborhoods, running back and forth until the streetlights came on once we came home from school, did our homework, and finished our chores. But not at school. I was petrified!!

It was the worst feeling in the world, waiting to be chosen yet always being the last to be chose. Being put in a position where you have to be picked, or chosen because you were thought to the best person for the job. Chosen because of what you bring to the table or left standing because you were not. But what happens when you are the runt of the litter? What happens when you are made to feel as if you are not good enough. This is the way I was made to feel in my junior high school years.

When you think about it, there is always someone who is bigger after all, taller, smarter or better than you. God made us all different. Different parts, each one significant as we make up the "body" of Christ. Why don't we feel like our part is as important as the next? Oh, the things that we tell ourselves and the impact that it has on us when we begin to buy into the thought of not being good enough.

You see it matters not whether the person who is telling you that you are not good enough is your voice or someone else's, the consequences of buying into the falsehoods of the enemy can have long-lasting effects on what God has called for you to do and the part that you playing in the building up of Gods kingdom. We must be careful of the voices for there are many. The Bible in John 10:27, tells us that *"My sheep know my voice and a stranger they will not follow."*

It is very important that we know and be confident in who we are as believers, and that we also see the value of who we are. Not with a prideful attitude, but with a spirit of humility acknowledging that we are nothing without God. A value based not on what we are or can do, but on what God can and will do and through us. It starts early.

As a child listening to what was not necessarily said but implied through the fact that I was always chosen last, caused me to question quite frequently who I was and if I were in fact good enough. What was it? Was it my clothes, was it my mannerisms, or could it be the way I wore my hair?

As the years progressed, I grew most found of music; and singing with groups, and choirs. It became my comfort zone. Never really wanting to be in the front, I always found myself migrating to the back. As I ponder the idea of always feeling as if I were last in life, I've come to realize as I searched the scripture that being last may not be such a bad thing after all. Look at David in 1st Samuel 16:6-13 NIV:

"When they arrived, Samuel saw Eliab and thought, "Surely the Lord's anointed stands here before the Lord." But the Lord said to Samuel, "Do not consider his appearance or his height, for I have rejected him. The Lord does not look at the things people look at. People look at the outward appearance, but the Lord looks at the heart." Then Jesse called Abinadab and had him pass in front of Samuel. But Samuel said, "The Lord has not chosen this one either." Jesse then had Shammah pass by, but Samuel said, "Nor has the Lord chosen this one." Jesse had seven of his sons pass before Samuel, but Samuel said to him, "The Lord has not chosen these." So, he asked Jesse, "Are these all the sons you have?" "There is still the youngest," Jesse answered. "He is tending the sheep." Samuel said, "Send for him; we will not sit down until he arrives." So, he sent for him and had him brought in. He was glowing with health and had a fine appearance and handsome features. Then the Lord said, "Rise and anoint him; this is the one."

It is made quite plainly in scripture that Man looks at the outside, but God looks at the heart. Learning to accept yourself in a world where most everything is dependent on outward appearances is a key to being confident in who you are. Unless we change our way of thinking, we will never rise above the negative image of ourselves that the enemy has so skillfully planted in your mind, before you know it, you have bought into what the enemy is feeding you.

So eventually, we end up thinking that we are not good enough, that we don't measure up at home, or in society. We may even begin to take on the behaviors of others all for the sake of fitting in. To feel like you belong. Think about it, if God wanted you to be someone else, then that's who he would you. These behaviors are unhealthy. In order to have a healthy image, we must base our self- image, no matter the situation, on what God says about us.

It's important that we learn to see ourselves the way God sees us. We are reminded in scripture of how David was initially not a consideration to become king, although He was being prepared for greatness throughout his entire life. There were so many reasons outwardly that David should not have been considered as king. But just like God did it for David, he has a way of turning things in our favor as well. Because David was chosen.

The things that God allows to happen in our lives may not feel good and may even seem insignificant or unfair. They sometimes even seem opposite to what we think. We must know that when we are obedient, and in the will of God, that no matter what storms blow in our life, that God is right there. Many are the afflictions of the righteous, but the Lord will deliver from them all. Like me, through my childhood, and early adulthood, I was made to feel so insignificant. There are times that you may feel worthless, or less than. This is when you must recall what your father says about you. Throughout my life I had to remind myself of who, and whose I was. Too many times, we are tempted to buy into what the enemy of our souls says of us.

The Word in John 10:10 warns us that "...*the enemy comes to steal to kill and to destroy.*" God emphatically tells us that He's *"come that we may have life and have it more abundantly."* Abundant life means living in the will, and the purposes of God.

I was one of those people who didn't look the part or dress the part. Like David, God called me from the back to the front. Out of darkness into His glorious light! Once this happened, I began to gain more confidence. Confidence to pray, and to sing in front of hundreds of people. God empowered me to do things that I would never have thought to do within my own power. I gained confidence, to preach and minister to God's people with the spirit of holy boldness. He did it for me, and for His glory.

So, I encourage you to not only know who you are, but be confident in who you are and allow God to do the rest. God is working in you.

Elder Janice Blackmon

CHAPTER 15
The Hole in My Soul
Janel Andrews

God never said our lives would be easy. In fact, he did say in Job 14:1 "Man that is born of a woman is of few days and full of trouble." (KJV), God knows what we are going through. It's a process. So, in spite of it keep praying, singing, praising and reading His Word. More importantly keep the line of communication between you and our father in heaven open!

At the age of 16, I lost my mom who at that time was the only parent in my home. I was the youngest of 6 siblings. All of whom were of adult age and living their adult lives. The passing of my mom hurt so much it literally felt as if I had a hole in my soul. It left me numb, speechless. I was scared, hurt, confused and mad.

How could God take my mommy from me? I was only 16. What was I to do? why me? All my other friends still had not only their mom but also their dad. He had already taken my dad from our home. Now He has taken my mom too and I will never see, hug, kiss or be able to talk to her ever again! It was at this moment that what I knew as childhood ended.

The guidance and assistance that I should have received from adult family members shifted to church members and friends for some of my family had the nerve to even tell me that I was the reason my mom passed away. I was told I would never have or be nothing. I was spoiled and because I was the one at home it was all my fault. So, for years and I mean *years* I carried that burden. Maybe it was my fault, maybe God was punishing me for something I did wrong.

Even at church I was being lied on so much. My dad thought I was the worst child on earth. It wasn't the children or young people it was the adults lying on me and about me. So, I stopped going to church. I turned to alcohol and partying. I was the life of the party for a while. The more I would drink the more I wouldn't have to feel like I was nothing. The more I drank the less pain of neglect I felt from the family and the adults who claimed they loved me and had my best interest at heart.

But you see, I was brought up in the church and I was taught how to pray at an early age. Thank God I had a praying Father, Aunt, and many others I can't even name who in spite of my downfalls continued to pray for me. Their prayers got me through one of the roughest times in my life. I slowly started to go back to church. I begin to pray and ask God to take the taste of alcohol from me. The more I prayed and attended church the less I wanted to drink and party.

This time it seemed different. This time my relationship with God was different. I continued to read and study His word. One of the things my daddy taught me was to always study to show yourself approved. Those old hymns he used to sing.... To where I used to sing them just because that's what we sung at church to me singing them now because I understood the meaning. They touched my soul.

As I look back over my life at the days of partying God was still with me even then. So, when I was wondering if he cared if I even existed. I now know that he did, and he still does. I say this to say no matter what you may go through in life continue to look up and seek God's face. Seek a relationship with the master for yourself. He will guide and keep you. I thank God for each trial He put before me. It helped to mold and shape me into the woman I am today.

Many of the people God used in the bible were people who were troubled, depressed, sick, etc. So, I know He can still use me and you too!
Proverbs 27:17 says *"Iron sharpeneth iron, so does a man sharpeneth the countenance of his friend."* I thank God for this opportunity to come before you today. As you read this know that nothing is impossible for God. There is not one person on this earth that has not encountered hurt, pain, disappointments, grief, loss, poverty, illness, etc. Keep pushing and praying. To God Be All Glory!

In His Service,
Janel Andrews

CHAPTER 16
It's Your Time
Tonya S. Jackson

One thing for certain in life, is that it has both its ups and downs. In reality, you have to keep promoting, be the best, love you, put things behind you and don't look back, even when your back is against the wall. In the beginning, trust God. In the middle, trust God. In the end, depend on God.

I have shared these motivational messages, to show that doubt, anxiety, worry, hurt will all come your way. They are a normal part of the flesh; the real battle is finding ways to replace those negative thoughts, feelings, and emotions with positive ones. These steps will help you in your journey to trust God completely. It's your time.

Keep Promoting.

Even if you get zero likes and no loves. Always promote your Church, your Talent, Ministry, or Keep Inspiring and Motivating others, because someone is watching! God can't trust a dormant leader. However, He can trust an on-fire Disciple. *#StayOnFireWithYourDreams.*

Either you are going to grow with some or outgrow them. You are NOT standing still for anyone. Those standing in your way, don't know you have wings. Surprise! God enlarges the harvest when you do the right things with the seed that He's supplied to you! Keep Planting!

On the flipside, you can't be moving fraudulently thinking you will get blessed in the end. And, let me say this, don't expect to be celebrated when you don't celebrate anyone. The truth is everybody needs encouragement, everybody needs somebody cheering them on, somebody that sees the best. You can be that person for the people in your life. And when you win against all odds, you'll understand why the enemy stacked so many of them against you. *#KeepGoing*

Be the Best You.

God made each and every one of us special. Don't apologize for who you are. Work hard to be the best version of yourself. If someone is uncomfortable with you; that's not your concern. Don't change just to please others. We weren't meant to be liked by everyone. Your individuality can be openly celebrated and enjoyed. Constantly seeking approval means you're worried that others are forming negative judgments of you. This steals the fun from your life. Flip the switch on this habit. Life is Short! Focus on your life ahead and free yourself from Satan's traps. It can be challenging but keep going. Continue to strive in all that you do*#YouAreGreatAsYouAre*

You Are About to Rise Up!
When you're a good person - the struggles are going to come - but so do the blessings. Be grateful even when everything doesn't always go your way. God always knows best. When you are up against the wall...fight your battles with prayer! Know this - Your call is greater than your fall! God supplies grace for your thorns!

Let yourself breathe. And don't punish yourself for stuff you did when you didn't know any better. Stop self-sabotaging yourself! Your time is coming! Continue to apply the hard work with your patience.

God is about to expose you and put you in the right position! Chin up. There is nothing wrong with you. This is just what living looks like sometimes! Relax and trust that things will work out. Let it go and trust God. He did it before! *#YourLifeIsGoingToBeGreat*

Love You, Even When...
When you love who you are, everything changes. You no longer seek validation and approval. You quit sending out energy of a need to be fulfilled from others. You become a powerful source within yourself! Don't be afraid of change for the better.

Be afraid of staying the same! When you're no longer able to change a situation, you're challenged to change yourself. It takes courage, discipline and focus. Seek your strength from God. Do it single-mindedly. You'll get there! And even if all doors seem closed and you feel like you're facing a dead end, God can and will provide alternative solutions to your problem.

Understand His Plan. Keep a look out for new opportunities. Often, we are so hung up on the closed doors that we fail to see what's there!
Side Note: Don't get upset with people for not giving you the things that they cannot even give to themselves. *#It'sYour life...Love You!*

Admit It.
Pray Over it. Be Done with It. When you can admit your wrong doings and rise above them; you have arrived! God knows when to send you exactly what you need! Don't give up because you've messed up! Flip Side: Don't drive yourself crazy, worried about others talking about your mistakes! Start Praying. See, you have to focus on who God created you to be; and they will have to just deal with it!

You are about to transition from being ridiculed, to being sought after! What's used against your life, is the same thing God will use to bless it. You on your way! Rejection turns into a blessing. *#YouAreOut*

It All Works Out.
Don't think, because it looks like others are winning, you're losing. That's

a poverty mentality! Trust... God has enough blessings for everyone! Don't spoil what you have, by wanting what you don't.

Remember, that what you now have, was once among the things you only hoped for. So... you are blessed! There's so much more to life than being painfully petty, holding jealousy and disliking someone.

If you choose to allow life to cause you to have a bad attitude, that's on you! And, only insecure people are bothered by those who are confident in themselves. .Be happy for others without envying them...Life offers you an endless amount of possibilities. Signing off: Never settle. All things work together for your good. And now that you know better, you can expect God's best. *#ThankYouGodForItAll.*

Put It Behind You.

Today, you are going to put everything not purposeful behind you! You are taking your eyes off your problems! Heal your mind and thoughts! You may feel broken, (about people and things), but you are not! It's not over! God is giving you your strength back! Rejected? It's ok. Talked about? It's ok. Unforgiven? It's ok.

You are about to be rescued! Your blessing is close! You will be happy again! You will be yourself again! God has just closed some doors for you, that you thought needed to remain open! *#SitBackandWatch.*

Love Yourself.

In life you're going to lose friends, family and others, but no matter who walks out of your life, never lose yourself. The most important thing to learn how to do, is to love yourself, even when you feel unloved by others! Your pain will never stop, until you stop giving pain to others. You can't control the outcome of every situation, nor can you control the thoughts and opinions of people.

But you can create boundaries that protects your peace. Your response to negative things: "If God is for me, who can be against me." Don't let anyone control how you feel about you, your ideas or your dreams. Learn to trust in yourself. Use the wisdom God has given to you. *#LearnHowToBeThereForYourself*

Not Mad.

Don't stay mad at them. Don't let bitterness and resentment take root in your heart. Their poison will harm your soul eventually. Let go of the hurt or hate that comes with it. Turn to God to heal you. Feel whole again with a much lighter heart! Side Note: Don't listen to the wrong crew.

Standing back from situations, gives you the perfect view. Right is right and Wrong is just wrong. But you have to be the better and move on! Know that disconnecting from certain people can bless your life! But if revenge is what you are seeking, you better dig two graves! *#CatchIt*

No Looking Back in 2020!

Allowing God to remove the negative things out of your life and replace it with positive outcomes. Everybody has a season...they should not judge you while you are in yours. Because condemnation is a trick of the enemy, that he tries to use when he knows God has already forgiven you.

The day you stop submitting your emotions to the negativity of others; is the day you'll be free. Positivity only upsets negativity.

This is the place you start looking over your year, to review the progress you've made since last year. This is the season people are about to realize they never knew who you really were.

Your scenery is about to change for the rest of 2020. God is about to lift you up and bring you out of suffocation! He is about to Bless you on purpose! Addressing the mess. Whatever you're going through, don't let it hold you down or let it govern the goodness in you. Stay Positive and Strong. *#NoMatterTheAttackYouCantTurnBack.*

Know Your Place with Others.

When you finally learn your place in people's lives, your feelings won't get hurt! That's one of the most important life lessons you'll learn. Whether it's friends, family or whomever. Just because you feel a certain way about them, doesn't mean they feel the same; no matter what you have done or how many times you may have been there for them.

Adjust yourself accordingly. And when people show you who they are, believe them and keep it moving! We'd all love to be selfless, but it becomes difficult around those who constantly hurt us. If people are bad for your mental health and consistently trigger negative emotional responses, hindering your growth, then go ahead and create a boundary.

And even when people mean you no Good, God will work it out for your Good! Side Note: You don't have to rebuild a relationship with everyone you've forgiven! You either walk around in Peace or Pieces! *#ChoosePeace*

Hear Ye.

When, not if, the Devil chases after you, keep running! When the Devil is on your back, keep shaking him. When the Devil likes confrontation, keep the peace. When the Devil doesn't understand your dedication to God, keep going! And yes, the demons will keep attacking you, trying to block and stop your progress; so be warned about this! No matter what we face, when we attempt to follow God's path, we will be safe.

Be tough, you are breaking through! May you get a sign this week that shows you that you're on the right path and that things are flowing and moving in your favor. May the sign be evident, clear, and direct. *#JesusWill*

Time Out.

Moving in silence is required in some things. You don't owe anyone an explanation for why you went ghost all of a sudden. Don't rush. Take some time to focus on you; and never settle. Some stuff you have to fix away from people's input. Take a "people-out" period.

The Flip Side: Things might make you cry but refuse to let it make you quit! Don't check out! Be present. And, you're not blind. You're just choosing to close your eyes to situations God is making plain for you.

Open your eyes, ears. Listen. God is telling you to lay low. Be strong! Refocus! A strong person is not the one who doesn't cry. A strong person is one who cries and sheds tears for the moment then gets up and fights again! You're working on yourself and trying to do better.
#YourVibeHasChanged!

It's your time,
Tonya S. Jackson

CHAPTER 17
It's Our Issue, Too
Minister Charlotte Walker

While sitting here, the word 'issues' befell my spirit. There seems to be one thing after the other that we are going through or have to deal with. Seemingly so overwhelming that we don't know what to do, or how we're going to make it through. Issues. We all have them. We can't run away, ignore or deny them. It's not how we react (impulsively) but how we respond (thought process, being rational, prayer guided). Meaning, it's how we handle them that decides our outcome or our *"come through!"*

Everyone may not be as strong as another person is when issues arise. Even as a Christian woman, when issues arise, I do sometimes feel the pressures of not knowing how I need to approach a certain situation. None of us are superhuman or super women. We are experiencing natural feelings and thoughts. But because I'm connected to the *True Vine*, I am reminded that my anchor is in HIM! We don't dwell, we take it to the WELL that NEVER RUNS DRY!

On this journey as a Christian woman, we sometimes allow selfishness, self-righteousness, yes, self-centered like it's all about us, we will even allow pride to seep in, which causes us to feel as though 'we' have are beyond hardships and will turn our heads when we see or know of someone else who might be having issues with life. Need I remind us that none of us have arrived!

You are blessed to be a blessing. It's up to us to make a difference. It's not about material things all the time. We must stop in our uppity Christian tracks and begin to ask what we can do to help others through? When we have reserves about assisting another, let's remember what Psalm 40:2 says: *"He brought me up also out of a horrible pit, out of the miry clay, and set my feet upon a rock and established my goings."*

Meditate on that word *also*. That's the reminder that God was your help and He probably sent someone to help you! I'm certain that HE DID! I'm telling God THANK YOU for bringing me up out of the pit.

It's nothing that we have done; God did it for us; He wants us to help others who may have the same or like issues we've had. As my aunt used to say, 'don't ever forget what God has done for you'! She would say 'when He brings you through, the only time you should look back is to tell Him 'thank you'; and when you see somebody who needs help' 'you help them because God helped you'! We as Christians need to be reminded that we were not born with the Bible in our hands reciting scriptures readily knowing that God will supply all our needs. That came with personal growth and our acceptance of Christ and believing in His Word.

It didn't separate us from having issues of life, but it gave us the wisdom and the knowledge to bring it all and lay it at His feet knowing that He would take care! What am I saying? There are people who don't pick up the Bible at all to read it. However, in us saying we are Christians they will observe what we do to see how we handle the issues of life. They are watching us to decide if they want to live the way we live and follow Christ.

I remember my husband and I were in Alexandria, Louisiana in the month of February of 2019. After just having a procedure done, we'd stopped by the store, he went in to get us something to drink. As I sat there waiting for him to come out, I noticed there was a young lady who looked to be about the age of 27, sitting in her car with her flashers on in front of the Walmart. She had a baby that appeared to be about 2 years old.

As a woman, and being the mother of four, and two of them are women about the same age, all I could think about was how I would want somebody to help my girls if it were them. The enemy tried to say, "don't you help her. Nobody helped you when you and your two older children were stranded on side of the road when your car broke down. Look at her... she's faking. You see that nice car she's driving and the way she's dressed? It's a trick."

You know the old cliche; "If it looks like a duck, swims like a duck, and quacks like a duck, then it probably is a duck." That wasn't the case this time. The devil works in bringing up stuff that happened over 27 years ago just so you won't do what God tells you to do. That's the mission of the enemy. We can't let him win. Just like he has a mission, we do, too. That's what we have to do. We have to show the devil that he's the real trick and that the joke is really on him! I said devil you don't run nothing here God is my Father and it is Him whom I serve!

I said to my husband, "Hun, pull over there and let's see what's going on." When we pulled over, the woman explained she'd been there visiting some friends over the weekend and her car was on empty and she'd run out of pampers for her baby. First thing we did was put gas in her car, buy her baby pampers, get them something to eat and prayed for her and with her for them to have a safe trip home before we left her.

We must be reminded that Jesus came to help, and since we're portraying to be "Christlike" let's follow the example that He set! We can't walk in the flesh when dealing with life's issues. Whether they are ours, or whether they belong to someone else that may need our help. Romans 8:4 says that *"The righteousness of the law might be fulfilled in us, who walk not after the flesh, but after the Spirit."* If it was left up to us, we would probably make the decision to keep going, but because we know what God says we should do, it compels us to be about our Father's business. I'm not telling you to take on everything and help everybody because some things we know the only thing that will help is prayer!

Use discernment because God will provide you with instruction and He will not send you into the enemy's camp. He will not allow you to go anywhere that is going to bring harm to you. But if God has given us resources or the means to help someone and it is beneficial to them help; you will find out that it was a part of your process to help someone else's' struggle. The glory belongs to God!

All throughout life we're presented with issues, pressures, struggles, tragedies and trials. These are lessons preparing us to pass the tests. Some of us have greater issues of tests and trials than others have. The Bible says in Matthew 17:20, *"Because of your unbelief, for assuredly, I say to you, if you have faith as a mustard seed, you will say to this mountain, 'Move from here to there,' and it will move; and nothing will be impossible for you."*

Therefore, no matter what we're tested with, there's no issue, pressurized enough to keep us in the struggle. Why? You do know when you walk by faith and not by sight? The foundation of our faith is solid in Christ! When issues arise remember the test was passed when Jesus paid it all at on the Cross at Calvary. Jesus has the touch to RELEASE THE PRESSURE! He stands at the door knocking for you to walk though and lay it all at His feet!

It's our duty to bear the infirmities of the weak because Jesus has prepared the way for the Christian journey of Faith and we find our strength through Him and in Him. We can help others bring it to Him by setting the example in the life we are living.

He says in Matthew 11:28-30, *"Come unto me, all ye that labor and are heavy laden, and I will give you rest. Take my yoke upon you and learn of me; for I am meek and lowly in heart: and ye shall find rest unto your souls. For my yoke is easy, and my burden is light."* In all of this, Jesus is saying NO PRESSURE!

And as I close this chapter, I leave you with this, when we become mature *faith walkers*, we leave behind focusing on the material things, we leave behind focusing on the time we may have to lose to help someone else.

We leave behind being worried about what someone may have done to us that causes us to not want to help them. We leave behind any negative thoughts. Why? Because our focus is on Jesus and doing what He would have us to do. It's a part of the charge He has given us to keep.

My question is, we as Christian women, are we keeping our charge? A last thought to ponder; if you know a sister is like a frail, thin branch on a tree and the branch is about to break, will you be that big branch in her time of need that will stretch out because you're a bit stronger at the time and bow over just a bit to help her hold on? My prayer is that we will all do that for one another. After all, our help comes from the Lord!

CHAPTER 18
Almost Homeless... But God
Charmaine Witherspoon

Ecclesiastes 3:1-8
(New King James Version)

To everything there is a season, A time for every purpose under heaven:

A time to be born, and a time to die;
A time to plant, and a time to pluck what is planted;
A time to kill, and a time to heal;
A time to break down, and a time to build up;
A time to weep, and a time to laugh;
A time to mourn, and a time to dance;
A time to cast away stones, and a time to gather stones;
A time to embrace, and a time to refrain from embracing;

A time to gain, and a time to lose;
A time to keep, and a time to throw away;
A time to tear, and a time to sew;
A time to keep silence, and a time to speak;
A time to love, and a time to hate;
A time of war, and a time of peace.

It was the year 2017 and I had a few months left of my year of service. Just that quick, a whole year had almost gone by and I survived it all. I moved all the way from Baltimore, MD to Phoenix, AZ to be the hands and feet of Jesus. I came to Phoenix to serve. It was one of the most rewarding years that now brings me so much joy. I still talk about my year of service to this day. It was truly life changing. Generally, before the end of a service year, most go into prayer to discern and ask God what they should do next? Others discern if God is calling them to another year. So, I did what I knew to do most, I went into prayer.

Ephesians 6:10-18
New King James Version (NKJV)
10 Finally, my brethren, be strong in the Lord and in the power of His might. 11 Put on the whole armor of God, that you may be able to stand against the [a]wiles of the devil. 12 For we do not wrestle against flesh and blood, but against principalities, against powers, against the rulers of [b]the darkness of this age, against spiritual hosts of

> *wickedness in the heavenly places. 13 Therefore, take up the whole armor of God, that you may be able to withstand in the evil day, and having done all, to stand. 14 Stand therefore, having girded your waist with truth, having put on the breastplate of righteousness, 15 and having shod your feet with the preparation of the gospel of peace; 16 above all, taking the shield of faith, with which you will be able to quench all the fiery darts of the wicked one. 17 And take the helmet of salvation, and the sword of the Spirit, which is the word of God; 18 praying always with all prayer and supplication in the Spirit, being watchful to this end with all perseverance and supplication for all the saints—*

The next three months were the hardest months that I've ever had to face. The organization that I had come to know, and love started to change right before my very eyes. There was a meeting a few months prior to when I left. This is one of the reasons I decided it was time for me to move on. The conversation was about the occult and the women that we serve. Should they or should they not be allowed to have tarot cards and things of the occult in their rooms? I immediately pushed back. I had a serious problem with it. The result of the meeting ended with "The IRS trumps Jesus."

There I heard it for myself funding was what they were after. But I thought Jesus was the reason why we did this? What about Jesus I thought? Who is going to be faced to deal with the spiritual implications of having things of the occult within our homes? The higher leaders don't have to live there but we do, as well as the women we serve. I was livid. Here, I fight in prayer every day for my home that I'm leading and now I have to deal with things of the occult because funding is necessary.

The only response was to let a Priest come in and bless the home. I left the meeting feeling shocked and speechless. The very thing that I loved so much has chosen finances over the WORD of GOD. But I thought it was the WORD that we stand on. Philippians 4:19 says *"But my God shall supply all your needs according to his riches in glory by Christ Jesus."*

What happened to trusting in Jesus for our finances? What happened to saying NO to having things of the occult in our homes? Needless to say, I stayed the course and finished my year of service until my time was done. I didn't break contract, but I did break down into prayer and fought until my time was done.

Proverbs 3:5-6
King James Version (KJV)

"Trust in the Lord with all thine heart; and lean not unto thine own understanding. In all thy ways acknowledge him, and he shall direct thy paths."

I felt the Holy Spirit leading me to stay in Phoenix after my year of service. But where would I go? Where would I live and where would I work? These and many others are the questions that I asked. I was obedient and said yes Lord but the next two months I faced were the toughest months that I've ever faced ever. God said stay and I said "Ok." But I didn't know what my future would hold or ultimately where I'd end up.

I was choosing to trust God and no one else. My mom, on the other hand, wanted me to come home. I had everything I ever needed at home; the comfort of my bed, the familiarity of my hometown, the vast amount of work opportunities and connections since I went to graduate school there and of course my lovely family. But I decided to take a risk with Jesus. I did that because the word of God says in Deuteronomy 31:6 New International Version (NIV) *"Be strong and courageous. Do not be afraid or terrified because of them, for the Lord your God goes with you; he will never leave you nor forsake you."* I knew deep down inside that if God wanted me to stay here, He would give me everything I'd need. For He is the Great Shepherd.

Psalms 23:1 *"The Lord is my Shepherd; I shall not want."*

Hebrews 11:1
King James Version (KJV)
"Now faith is the substance of things hoped for, the evidence of things not seen."

Now that I believed that God wanted me to stay in this new town, I was required to have the faith that He would supply my every need. It now became the time to put my faith into action. James 2:26 says:
"For as the body without the spirit is dead, so faith without works is dead also."

So, I started applying for jobs and looking for housing options about a month or so before my contract was up on August 31st. During my time applying for jobs and housing options, I had an interesting idea to bring about a proposal to the organization.

The proposal included starting an aftercare program for the missionaries in exchange for housing to help them get back on their feet. After all, I had a Master of Social Work degree, so I decided to put my degree to good use.

The proposal included things like volunteering for free for 3 months in exchange for a place to live at the day off house while I worked on finding a job. I typed it up and gave the submission to my supervisor who said they would hand it over to someone who'd be willing to take a look at it. I was overjoyed but not relieved. I really hoped that this to work. I was using every ounce of faith I had because honestly, I didn't know what to do. I applied for job after job in hopes that someone would pick me up quick so that I could start working but nothing happened.

Sometime later, I received a response back from my supervisor and was told that they couldn't start such a program at this time. I was hurt. After all, the day off house, sat vacant when the missionaries weren't there and it was more than enough room. So, I went into prayer. Just about every chance I got, I was in the chapel, praying and crying out to God` in tears but I knew in my heart the Holy Spirit wanted me to stay but I felt like I didn't have any options and my contract expiration date was near. I went from belief to disbelief, to being hurt, worried, upset and frustrated. Until one day, the day in which I decided that I was just going to trust God fully.

Every Monday night, when the staff and the moms had dinner, I went around and said how much I believed God will help me find a place and a job very soon. Everyone was in agreement, but no one had a clue of the stress I was under. Trying to find your own way in a seemingly unknown town is hard but with no car, no job and no housing, it makes it even more difficult.

I was a few weeks away from my contract date and I still had nothing tangible. The only thing I had to rely on was the Word of God. I had a friend who offered to let me stay with her but when the time actually came for me to move; she was nowhere to be found. Every phone call went to voicemail, call backs went to voicemail, I never was able to reach her. I reached out to my supervisor one last time asking for help. The organization offered me 2 weeks after my contract date was up to stay at the day off house but nothing else. There were no services, no resources, just me and my faith. I agreed and my anxiety grew even more. But prayer was still on my lips as I was about to face the inevitable: Homelessness.

Romans 8:28,
"And we know that all things work together for good to those who love God, to those who are the called according to His purpose."

A few days before I moved into the day off home that the organization had offered me, I received a phone call. It was an employer. They wanted to interview me. Excitement was what I felt but anxiety shortly took over because I had no way there. After making some calls and helping out the new missionaries, I was able to borrow their day off car; the one with no A/C and it was about 120 degrees outside.

I arrived at the interview site about 4 minutes to my interview time, dripping in sweat, carrying a colorful folder with my resume in hand. The security guard gave me a bottle of water and I had about a 10-minute wait for the interviewer to show up which gave me some time to relax and not look disgruntled.

I interviewed, dropped the car off and walked to the day off house which was just a few short blocks from where I dropped the car off and prayed. The next day I was hired. My contract ended on August 31st and I was hired the first week of September.

I received a phone call from an old employee of the organization who let me know she knew someone who needed someone to take over her lease.

Everything was pretty much paid for during the month of September so all I had to do was move in and pay a small fee. I met up with the woman, saw the place and a few days later, signed the papers. I had just rented my very first room in an off-campus apartment complex close to Arizona State University.

In just two weeks, Jesus had turned my life completely upside down for the better. No longer was I 2 weeks away from being Homeless but I was moved in and working before the 2-week deadline and was able to pay my rent which included all utilities by the 1st of October. Needless to say, I only use a few days of the 2-week period that the organization gave me. When I tell you that Jesus will do it, He will! As the song says, "He may not come when you want Him, but he'll be there right on time. He's an on-time God. Yes, He is!"

CHAPTER 19
Forgiveness
Marlo Eggerson

Colossians 1:13-14
"For he has rescued us from the kingdom of darkness and transferred us into the Kingdom of his son, who purchased our freedom and forgave our sins."

My name is Marlo Eggerson. I am a mother, a wife of a God-fearing husband and a member of Redemptive Word Church. If I spoke one word to you, you would get a mixture of my northern and southern twang. I am originally from Racine Wisconsin. I currently reside in Amarillo, Texas. For a few minutes today, I would like to draw your attention to the word "forgiveness."

What does the word forgiveness mean to you? Have you had to forgive yourself? The dictionary definition of forgiveness is: The action or process of forgiving or being forgiven. Forgiveness is the international and voluntary process by which a victim undergoes a change in feelings and attitude regarding an offense and overcomes negative emotions such as resentment and vengeance.

How many times have we forgiven others for things they have done towards us? Or maybe things they have said about us. There was a time when I was still in the world where if you had done or said anything about me, forgiveness was the furthest thing from my mind. In fact, I was ready to lay hands on you and not Holy hands either. I know some of us at one time wanted to go there, I'm not the only one.

Now that I've come into the knowledge of Jesus Christ and I allow the Word of God to lead me, forgiveness has taken on a new meaning for me. Forgiveness is dismissing your demand that others owe you something, especially when they fail to meet your expectations, failed to keep a promise and failed to treat you justly.

Jesus said in Matthew 5:39 *"If someone strikes you on the right cheek, turn to them the other also."* What this scripture says to me is that instead of lowering myself through acts of aggression or retaliation, I will forgive those who offend me. It did not matter what the offense was. It did not even matter who it was that offended me. But what about forgiving yourself?

The Bible teaches us in 1 John 1:9: *"If we confess our sins, He is faithful and just to forgive us our sins, and to cleanse us from all unrighteousness."*

Now friends please don't do as I did and beat yourself up. I used to think that I had to remember all my sins and I would go to God all day, every day, each time I would remember something I had did or done to someone else.

I could picture Jesus saying, "Someone disconnect her main line because this child of mine keeps asking for what has already been given." He had already taken my sins with Him to the Cross.

So how do I forgive myself? I still felt bad for all the terrible things I had done to my body. I felt even worse for the humiliation I put my family through. Everyone was telling me it was ok and that they still loved me. However, in my mind that wasn't enough.

I knew God had already forgiven me, but maybe he was wrong because I don't feel I deserve forgiveness. Maybe Christ's sacrifice on the cross may not have been enough to cleanse me of my sins. Maybe I need to do more to make up for what I feel is lacking in Jesus's sacrifice. So, I thought I would "HELP" Him with His sacrifice for me by volunteering for everything. I would attend every meeting at church whether it had something to do with me or not. I just said yes to everything until one day I just crashed and burned out. Silly me. Not forgiving myself made me feel like I was being humble in the eyes of God.

What I failed to realize is I was being distracted by past transgressions instead of being focused on God. You all remember in the book of Matthew when Jesus walked on the water. When the disciples saw him, it was Peter who said,

"If it is truly you, tell me to come to you on the water." Said Peter.
Jesus replied, "Come." and Peter came out of the boat into the water and started walking towards Him. Then Peter noticed the storm, became afraid and began to sink. He cried out for Jesus to help and immediately Jesus caught him. "You of little faith," He said, "Why did you doubt?"

What it made me realize is that God was calling to me saying you are forgiven, but all the wrong I did in the past kept raging up against me like a storm. That storm distracted me, it kept me in fear, and I began to sink in the fear that I was not forgiven. And all the while what I needed to do was to stay focused on the promise that God has truly forgiven me.

The Scriptures tell us that *"He has rescued us"* and refers to the believer's spiritual liberation by God from Satan's kingdom. So, to go around forgiving others, but secretly holding on to things you feel you've done to yourself in your past, is walking around in darkness which is Satan's Kingdom. The enemy wants you to hold on to the thought that you can't forgive yourself and even make you doubt that God has forgiven you. It is doubt that will taint your faith. The devil wants us to have that fear. He will hang that over you if you let him. We are taught to forgive others when they trespass against us and seek forgiveness.

When we ask for God's forgiveness based upon Christ having already paid for our sins and our trust in Him as Savior and Lord, He forgives us. However, even though we are released from the bondage to sin, we can still choose to wallow in it and act as though we are not freed from it. Likewise, with guilty feelings we can accept the fact that we are forgiven in Christ, or we can believe the devil's lie that we are still guilty and should therefore feel guilty.

The Bible says that when God forgives us, *"He remembers our sins no more"* according to Jeremiah 31:34. When our former sins come to mind, we can choose to dwell upon them, or we can choose to fill our minds with thoughts of the awesome God who forgave us and thank and praise Him for it. Remembering our sins is only beneficial when it reminds us of the extent of God's forgiveness and makes it easier for us to forgive others and ourselves. This is also useful when others try to bring up your past as well.

After I learned how to forgive myself. I repented and not repeated. I am so grateful for God's prevenient grace. I learned how to show love to myself. I am not my own. My prayer life changed. My health became my priority. I live my life knowing that if I fall it's ok. God is not expecting me to live for the world, He wants me to live for Him.

Forgiveness is good for You and me. It's good for the heart, mind and soul. In closing, forgiving yourself is not about forgetting, not about bringing the past up to yourself or others in negative ways.

Forgiveness is simply letting go of what is holding you back so you can move forward with God. Forgiving yourself for whatever hurt or harm you may have caused is a gift. You must only do it once. If God has moved, on shouldn't we do the same?

CHAPTER 20
Attraversiamo
Angela Foster

Isaiah 30:21
"When you turn to the right or turn to the left, you will hear his voice behind you to guide you, saying, this is the right path; follow it."

Every year since 2015 I have posted this painting on my social media page. Not necessarily at the same time each year but at some point, during the year I have found some new reason to reflect on this picture. But today I am finishing up some reading in Habakkuk 2:4, where God says, *"But the righteous shall live by faith."*

As I pondered, I looked up from my reading to see that the picture seemed closer to me than ever. I felt like I was standing there again. I was flooded with the memories of the actual time I was standing on the edge of here and there.

It was there, at the park in which I have visited many times in the past. I have walked with my children and friends around the lake. Taking in its beauty during various seasons observing the water levels which indicted if we were in a drought season or a season full of rain and moisture.

Living in the panhandle of Texas makes us vulnerable to all kinds of weather, and seasons of drought were not uncommon. But this year, in June of 2015, it was not a drought season at all. I can't recall how much rain we experienced that year, but our little lake was glistening with the sun shining on the water like mini flashlights. The landscape was bursting with green.

Our trees don't get as tall as those from the east coast of the United States where I grew up. No, these green trees, even though they look like healthy stalks of broccoli, appeared to be in full bloom. And the grass was almost velvety. Not tall grass; but short, soft and plush.

It was beautiful day. Simply beautiful. I recall the warm air was perfect. It wasn't that scorcher air as it tends to be in June and there was barely any wind at all. In this area it was rare to enjoy a day of sun, mild temperatures and no wind all at once. This was one of those rare days.

I remember the details for one because it was Father's Day. It was Father's Day and I was making laps around the lake while my children spent time with their dad without me. It was a rare day indeed. A day I had to decide to stay or go.

Do I walk away from my marriage of over 30 years or do I try one more time? The warmth of the sun, the beautiful landscape and the sound of rushing water was the perfect picture of how I was feeling in the depth of my being. I had some sense of warmth and comfort, yet my thoughts were rushing from the recesses of my mind. You know, the Christian thoughts. Divorce is a sin.

Have you given it enough time? You've been through way too much! And will my kids ever forgive me? I made my way to a shady area and sat on a bench near one of the bridge crossings over the lake. As I stared at the bridge my own thoughts were interrupted as I watched in terror as parents let their children run across it. They could have easily fallen through the widely spaced railing and into the lake. But oddly enough they didn't. Some ran, then stopped and peered over, and some just slowly walked across.

As I sat there on that bench observing what I considered the recklessness of parents and the freedom of children, I felt drawn to the bridge. I took the long way around and found myself standing at the start of the walkover bridge. Please understand, this bridge is not a great wonder. It isn't very high, nor is it very wide. It was pretty sturdy made of iron and concrete. And the lake below as beautiful as it looked and sounded, was not ocean deep no anywhere near the depth of the Great Lakes, so I should not have been afraid. But I could not move. I was frozen.

I pondered almost every detail of my life from past to present. I had so much uncertainty! I was being thrust into a life I didn't know anything about. But who really knows what life is about but God! I stood there, tears running down my face and I heard the Lord's voice so clearly say to me, "ATTRAVERSIAMO!"

Attraversiamo was a word I had become very fond of from a book I'd read several years before. It is Italian for "Let's cross over" as in, let's cross over to the other side. LET'S CROSS OVER?

But I couldn't. I looked straight ahead. I could see the end but the journey from where I was to where I needed to be was terrifying. I heard Him tell me to crossover to the other side.

The other side of pain, the other side of hurt, the other side of disappointment. But all I could think of is what would happen to me on the way over? I could slip, or if someone ran by me, they could knock me over the edge. What would happen if I got halfway across and couldn't make it? I would be too far to turn back and not far enough to end this thing!

That warmth in the depth of me was resonating with what I heard the Lord say, "Let's cross over." He wasn't telling me to take one step by myself. He was saying, "You will not be alone! Every step of the way, I will be with you."

He knew what this word *Attraversiamo* meant to me. He knew that I have always needed and wanted Him to be with me. And now He was assuring me that the decision I needed to make would not be done alone. And with that, I moved my feet, one step at a time; with tears rolling down my face, I crossed over! I crossed over to the other side. Yet, I stood there for a moment, not moving, and then I looked back.

I looked back to see what I had accomplished. There are so many times we have been told, not to look back. Just keep going. I think that may work in some cases when looking back holds you back. But for me looking back was catapulting me forward. I was so excited that I skipped back over the bridge to the beginning of the crossover and snapped a photo of it and for one final trek across I power walked to the other side. I'll admit, I didn't have all the answers to my questions, but my heart was no longer heavy.

I knew I wasn't alone. I knew the Lord was going to be with me. I knew the same faith it took to believe in God, was the faith I was going to need to help me, guide me, and lead me through to every "other side" moment I would face. I would face a multitude of "other side" moments since then. Those moments have moved me from pain to hope, from chaos to joy, and from disappointment to faith.

Faith. That's how this whole journey started. I have found that it always starts here, with faith. Faith is not a religious word. It is a life word. We use faith all the time. We get on airplanes, ride elevators, get married, raise children, and the all famous example, we sit in chairs!

The question of the century is, what is our faith in? The pilot? The mechanism? Our spouse? Our abilities? Or the idea? In each one of these common example's faith is exercised.

I have chosen to have faith in God and His Word. The Bible is my instruction manual and my encouragement regarding life and faith.

With these examples we can live by faith. Hebrews 11:6 says, *"Without faith it is impossible to please God."* Then 2 Corinthians 5:7 reminds us that *"We walk by faith not by sight."* And in Hebrews 10:23 for *"He Who promised is faithful."* And as my reflection began, I remembered Habakkuk 2:4 which says *"The righteous live by faith."*

This painting, *Attraversiamo*, was painted by my son Landon Lee Foster Jr. That day after the crossover I went directly home, showed him the photo I'd taken and said, "Son, I need you to paint this picture." He was just getting started in his painting endeavors. I felt like Mary, the mother of Jesus that day when she explained to Jesus that there was no more wine for the wedding. She didn't ask Him any questions. She knew His potential and just directed others to do what He said.

I knew my son's potential, but I had no idea this painting would provoke deep thoughts and influence many changes and redirection over time. When I lifted my eyes and raised my head from the text in Habakkuk and looked at the painting in front of me, I was there at the bridge needing to make a few more changes or better stated, adjustments in my life.

Some things must go, and some things just need to be restructured. This time when I looked at the painting, I noticed in the midst of all the accuracies, the placement of every tree, cloud and every reflection, there was one thing not pictured. It was the path at the end of the bridge. Upon this discovery I burst in tears. Not because I thought my son had forgotten to paint it. He only painted what he saw.

At times, I forget, and this was one of those times. I often forget there is a path after the crossover! It isn't hard to find if I just keep walking. The Lord always provides a path with the crossover. If he didn't provide a way, if He didn't provide a path, it would be as if He has forsaken us and left us without direction. But because of my faith in Him and His Word, He promised that He would never leave us or forsake us. And I believe this truth, according to Deuteronomy 31:6-8 and Hebrews 13:5.

The path is before me. For every crossover there is a path to be taken to move from where I am to where I need to be and where the Lord wants me to be. I have a tendency to want to see where the path is leading me. But this is where faith comes in. If the righteous live by faith, then it is up to me to live by moving my feet toward the things I know and the adventures I don't know.

It doesn't have to be complicated. Isaiah 30:21 makes it pretty simple. *"When you turn to the right or turn to the left, you will hear his voice behind you to guide you, saying, this is the right path; follow it."* I must remember the Lord's voice when He spoke to me, to guide me, Attraversiamo! LET'S CROSSOVER! For this is the path, now I must follow it in faith. Afterall, faith follows God!

Queens Supporting Queens

CHAPTER 21
Finding Your Purpose After 40
Keywana Wright

Ecclesiastes 3:1
"There is a time for everything, and a season for every activity under the heavens."

Have you ever found yourself living in a web of routines? Everyday seems to be predictable. Have you ever felt like you lost your purpose? You were busy doing works in the church, but not operating in your purpose? You were settled in a career that allowed you to live a decent lifestyle. However, something seemed to be missing in your life. I felt a sense of emptiness.

The road I was traveling spiritually had become familiar. I had grown content where I was. Deep inside I knew I had a purpose. I cried out to the Lord what is my purpose? Lord show me my purpose.

In the book of Ezekiel 37, God instructed Ezekiel to speak to the dry bones and they would come to life. God said "Keywana, I need you to speak life to some promises I gave you. I know the promises seem dead and years have gone by. Trust me; My word is true." God is not a man, that he should lie; neither the son of man, that he should repent: hath he said, and shall he not do it? Or hath he spoken, and he shall he not make it good? Numbers 23:19 says, *"I allowed you to go through some season. In order to prepare you for your purpose."*

On June 12, 2018, my purpose came to fruition. I wrote my first book, *Walking in God's Destiny*. How God turned my fear into faith? I begin studying God's word. One scripture I quoted often was, "Now faith is the substance of things hoped for and the evidence of things not seen". (Hebrews 11:11) I asked myself what am I hoping for? The bible says and without faith, it is impossible to please him, for he who comes to God must believer that he is rewarder of those who seek him.

It was through seeking God my purpose was rekindle and birthed. I began writing when I was 16 years old at a time when my parents separated and divorced. I began writing poetry to express my feelings of how I felt when my parents separated. My writing skills led me to write for our local newspaper in the section entitled "Word up! It was a section where high school student could write in the local newspaper weekly. I wrote for a year. I wrote many poems and prayers. My second book entitled " Keywana' s Collections of Prayers and Poems. I decided to publish my collections of work, I wrote years ago.

As I continued to seek God, He was revealing the plan He had for me. Jeremiah 29:11-12, *"For I know the plans I have for you plans to give you hope and a future. Then you will call on me and come and pray to me, and I will be found you, declares the Lord, and will bring you back from captivity."* God brought me out of my captivity, and I walked into my purpose.

When I turned 40 years old on August 30, 2018, my purpose of teaching people how to journal their prayers and pray intentionally became reality. To encourage people through my devotional writings. To teach others how to speak affirmations in their lives. I am still seeking God today. God doesn't always give you all the vision at one time. He reveals it in part. On December 19, 2019, I earned a Certificate of Biblical Leadership. As I continue my journey to fulfill my purpose and the calling upon my life, I am blessed to serve in Women's Outreach Ministry. I will continue to seek God, to study the word of God, and to work the plan he has given me.

There are three things you can do to help you discover your purpose too.

1. **Seek God**-Psalm 63," *O God, thou art my God; early I will seek thee."*

2. **Study the Word of God**-2 Timothy 2:15," *Study to shew thyself approved unto God, a workman that needed not to be ashamed, rightly diving the word of truth".*

3. **Work the plan**-James 2:18, *"But someone will say, you have faith, and I have works. Show me your faith without your works, and I will show you my faith by my works."*

It doesn't matter your age God has a plan for you.

We all have a purpose. God created us all for his divine purpose and plan.

Let's pray,

Dear God, we thank You for this day you have made. We pray for Your will to be done. Father, we know You have a plan for us. I pray that You will reveal the plans to the individuals, who are seeking you. The bible says" God has a plan to prosper us and to give us an expected end. We look to you Lord; we know our help comes from you. In Jesus Name, Amen.

CHAPTER 22
The Power in Being Weak
Jonetta Baggett

Did you know that being weak is a delight to the Lord? In 2nd Corinthians 12:9 NLT Paul stated that when he was given many revelations and was able to reach the 3rd heaven he had the opportunity to BOAST in what God had done and revealed, but he chose to only BOAST about his weaknesses. Paul said that he was given a 'thorn' in his side so that he would stay humble.

What is a 'thorn' in your life that instead of you keeping it intimate between Jesus Christ and yourself, you are posting to Facebook, bragging on Snap Chat, and telling anyone that is willing to listen? We need a crowd or validation from someone or something to feel that our so-called thorn at the time needs to be heard or felt. Wrong Sis!! Wrong Bro!! What is wrong with you being weak in silence? What is wrong with you truly giving your situation to Jesus Christ and not trying to figure it out, analyze it, take it apart, multiply and divide it?

Why do YOU have to be strong ALL the TIME? I know what you might say "I was built like this" or "This is all I know how to do" or the most used one "If I don't do it, then who will". Jesus will that's who. There are races that have passed down proudly from generation to generation that you are to be in a class all your own just because you are strong.

In 2nd Corinthians when Paul was trying to get out of his "thorn" and begged God to take it away he responded by saying "My grace is all you need. My power works best in weakness." This is all God wants us to be is weak. We must learn that while we are traveling this road of life that the creator has already created the path and it will come to pass. You, however, must know that while traveling down your ordained road use your "thorn" as a connection between Jesus and you. Life is not easy. Life is not fair and there is pain out here that you cannot control. The JOY and the PEACE that we get from Jesus Christ when we just let his will be done. Don't step in, don't talk about it just pray over it as it is being revealed and watch how your inner spiritual mind takes a deep breath. Inhale then Exhale the stress away.

I remember being at a place in my life that everyone near and far depended on me and being weak was not in the plan. You know the list of a woman's busy life that includes; motherhood, friendships, working daily, church meetings, children outings and the list can go on and on. We become so acclimated to this lifestyle that we never just sit down unless it's time to go to sleep and even then, we are thinking and asking ourselves "What do I have to do tomorrow?"

Let me remind you that yes this is part of your duty as a woman however, if you are always going and never really resting when do you have time to allow your spiritual mind to even exhale? This will cause you to run until the Lord almighty will sit you down! You know those "let me lay down for 30 mins." and then it turns into 4 hrs. of a well-rested nap. I want you to learn that it is okay to say NO! I know it's hard, it may even feel weird and family may disagree but you cannot be the Proverbs 31 woman if you do not allow yourself to be weak? Her weakness was seeking God as soon as she rose early every morning. She casted her cares, her concerns and family all to him and then she asked him what he wanted her to do that day.

The history of a woman is beyond us. There is history that we haven't even been told of or even tapped into because were too busy living for the right now moments. We're not sitting down to determine how our children or family would view me when I'm gone? How are we changing our toxic generational curses? Specifically, sometimes the African American woman is known for being so strong and carrying her family and because of this, we have allowed it to consume us to a point that we are a brick inside.

We won't let anyone in and the moment we decide to, we have a million bricks up and we are scared, we are cautious, we are angry, and sometimes even bitter because the last person that hurt you before you didn't allow yourself to heal. You must ask yourself what you are feeding my family mentally and spiritually? Promise yourself that in your seasons of being weak that it is your hibernation season and you will be better for not only yourself but for your family. It's time that we let that angry black woman stereotype die. Brothers, your sisters love you.

We want you to understand that it is okay for you to show your emotions. It's okay to share how you feel. Society has made it look like that the only man that can share his feelings is if he is LGBTQ. All men have this right. When does he release his stress, when can he be weak? Society doesn't want him to be. Sisters we must help our brothers release their stress so that they can continue to lead us. During hibernation season a bear preps all year long until it is time for hiding. They ensure that they have enough food to last a full 3 to 4 months before they come out again. We must remember to do the same in this season of our life. Don't wait until it's too late and now you're tired, depressed, and want God to fix it fast. Prepare yourself through the months to allow Jesus to direct your every move and when the enemy attempts to attack, you can so strongly throw your hands up and say Jesus it's your turn!

So, I know you may be wondering what I do after I have gained my strength? Stay humble! Stay in the place of Proverbs 31. I know you may not be a wife however she is the model woman for us to copy throughout life. I would hope eventually a man will find his good thing in you.

In the hibernation season you are slowly shaping yourself into being genuinely happy, genuinely seeking Jesus Christ in all things and in all things he will provide. Now sis, this will also be a trying time for you. Yes, we have to talk about this because it happens. The ugly face of the devil will try his best to get you off the course of hibernation. Do you know why? Because he sees the future too. His job has never changed, and it will
always remain the same, however remember JESUS CHRIST created him as well. So, don't take any of the strength you are gaining to just give it away to the enemy. You take your earned strength and use it as Jesus wants you to.

You are beautiful, you are classy, you are prayerful, and Jesus is intentional. Walk in that purpose with humbleness in your heart and mind, Jesus will adore you for your faithfulness. From day to day you may fill defeated or maybe even not worthy to live, But I must tell you that every day that Jehovah tells you to rise, you rise and go forth. Don't you dare get to a place of being so weak that you are not seeking the one who created you!!

Start this new journey with a journal of some sort. Write down your good days and write down your bad days. You don't have to do a long paragraph. Just write one sentence a day about how you felt and how you handled your day. It will start to become a necessary part of your life. What this will do is help you see how you handle life from day to day. You will then ensure that the day before is better. You will learn what to give energy to and what not to. You will start knowing who is toxic in your life and they must be removed. You will have a new-found respect for quiet time.

Start mediation before resting at night. This will cause your body, mind and your spiritual mind to connect to Jesus intimately. Get to know him on another level. You know what to do sis, just walk on over to hibernation lane and cast your cares to Jehovah. You've Got This!

Signed,
Jonetta Baggett
Restored Warrior

CHAPTER 23
Unmasking the Authentic Queen Within
Angela Lucas

Psalm 139:14 KJV
"I will praise You because I am fearfully and wonderfully made; marvelous are Thy works; and that my soul knoweth right well."

As women we often are more concerned about what people think of us if we don't have the house on the hill, the car, the job, the education and the perfect husband and kids. And let's not forget about the perfect body, pretty face, designer clothes and shoes. In all transparency, I have personally dealt with the different masks or facades. In this chapter you will discover God's purpose and inspiration in being who God has designed for women to become. We will also talk about the purpose and destiny that He desires Queens to acquire.

In order to discover who God has destined and purposed for us to become, we as women must unmask ourselves and expose our true identities. In other words, God's Word is stating in Psalm 139:14, Queen you are made like a beautiful flower, knitted together and wonderfully designed with love and care by God.

How do you feel when you are wearing these masks? And do you want to stop wearing them? Do you find yourself wondering how friends and family will act if you show them the real you? Queen you must not be afraid of how people perceive you. People often want the freedom to be themselves. But in most instances, they fear rejection or disapproval which drives them to compromise their true identity.

As you take the necessary steps to unmask your true identity, start by honestly asking yourself these questions:

1. Ask yourself does anyone know the *real you*?
2. What is the true reason you are hiding behind a mask instead of becoming who God has designed you to be?
3. Do you feel a sense of safety in wearing masks? Would you like to make a change?

Here are some answers I applied to unmasking myself I pray you find these helpful and useful as you begin to *Unmask the Authentic Queen in You*!
1. Examine your reasons why you feel the need to please others rather than yourself, and God.
2. Establish a closer relationship with God and other like-mined positive women for help and guidance.
3. Understand it is a process and establish a closer relationship and start with small steps toward becoming the Authentic Queen within you!

A popular quote (from an unknown source) states "We must feel loved for who we really are and not for what we pretend to be behind our many masks." Below are a few masks that I wore. I pray you can relate to these masks within yourself as you Unmask the Authentic Queen in You.

The Mask of Rejection
Perhaps you were rejected as a child by a parent. Maybe you were rejected by friends, or husband.
The Mask of Pain
This may include hurt from a divorce. You may be left feeling unwanted.
The Mask of Shame
This may be related to your self-confidence. You may have suffered exposure. You may have suffered a blow to your pride because of the lack of material possessions, such as designer clothes and shoes, etc. We often think these things give us greater value.

Now I will give you a few nuggets of wisdom on how to Unmask the Queen Within You:
1. Accept yourself for who you are.
2. Support your self-esteem.
3. Act on your personal beliefs and values regarding *you*.
4. Put time into your personal growth.
5. Rediscover who you belong to and who you are in the earth realm.
6. Embark on brand new visions, missions and plans for yourself.
7. Set small goals. These short-term and long-term goals should be measurable and obtainable.

Read Scriptures:
Ephesians: 2:10 "You are God's masterpiece."
Psalm: 139:14 "You are fearfully and wonderfully made."
Proverbs: 31:25 "She is clothed with strength and dignity."
Jeremiah: 29:11 "For I know the plans I have for you."

As I end this chapter, my prayer is for you Queen to examine the words and my personal experience to the surface and root of your heart. And you may heal and unmask the beautiful Queen in you. For my sister know that you are a Designer's original crafted by the loving hand of God. My prayer today is that you shall become the Daughter of God that he has destined for you to be Queen. Unmask yourself and begin to walk in your designed assignment.

Signed,
Queen Lady Angela Lucas

CHAPTER 24
We Are Better Together
Lakisha Sewell, MS

"She thinks she's something." She tries too hard to fit in." "Did you see what she had on?" "Girl, stop!" "Didn't she already wear that before?" "I heard her husband is cheating on her." "I don't like her", I wouldn't trust her around your man." "She doesn't support me, so I am not supporting her."
You get the point; we can be extremely hard on one another as women. I have learned over time; we are better together. I understand we all want to be recognized as an individual sometimes, but when we build together, we get there faster. As a mental health professional, I have always loved group therapy.

I instill in my clients the importance of peer support. For many people "groups help people feel like they are not alone, and it can be a collectively healing experience," according to Dr. Nakieta Lankster Psy D., a clinical psychologist who has a private practice in Demopolis, AL and Baltimore, MD. Personally, I find it to be more effective because we have an accountability to the group. We hold one another accountable. We do not enable one another. We want to see progress within our circle. We are not afraid to provide redirections. We are not offended when we are redirected. Also, we are not alone in our life struggles. I find it to be very therapeutic. On days when I am not feeling my best, I go to work knowing my day is about to get better. It is all in your attitude and how you perceive things.

Having a group of positive people cheering for you, gives you hope for this sometimes disruptive and cruel world. When we are a part of a successful group and every member does their part, we all win. We become a movement. Collectively, we are one; one in Christ. One body but many members.

"For as the body is one, and hath many members, and all the members of that one body, being many, are one body: so also, is Christ." 1 Corinthians 12:12 KJV.

Together we offer hope, encouragement, inspiration, and sometimes shared ideas. The problems come in when we allow the enemy to distract us from our common goal. We begin to compete with one another. As the saying goes, we become crabs in a bucket. There's nothing like seeing another queen win. It's very inspiring to me to be able to cheer for someone from within a crowd. This means the world to me. I tend to say often, I'm the hype man. I love to scream. It's like God gave me all these weird noises in my throat so I can scream for someone else. I cannot sing, but I love karaoke. I love supporting and motivating others.

I remember when my friend from college went to California to attend graduate school to receive her doctorate in Psychology. I stayed locally to receive my master's in counseling psychology
from The University of West Alabama. She wanted to become a Psychologist. When she called me to tell me she was graduating, I literally felt like I had completed my PHD as well! I told everyone that my friend is a doctor and I did not care how many times I said it and whom I said it too. I was extremely and naturally happy for her. Being happy for an individual is something that is common to me. Learn to cheer for people when it's not your winning season. We will have our time to win and until that season comes, help someone accomplish their goals. I promise, it will make you feel proud of who you are.

How can we as women get together without drama? We must pray first. We ask God to send us people who loves Him and have common goals. See the thing is, we can have different mission, but have common goals. We can still be beneficial to one another. We may have different methods but the common goals can be the same. First instance, if Susie wants to go out to the Salvation Army to offer service. She talks to her friends about it. Her friends get excited because they would like to do the same thing but withdraw from helping her because Susie said it first. Why would you allow that to stop you from teaming up to reach a common goal? Because you didn't say it first? Or because you don't want her to succeed because she would get recognition. Either way, Susie will do it and it may be harder for her to do it alone, but it will get done.

Let's say her friends would have helped her by adding their creativity and guidance, the community service would have been completed quicker. The bottom line, it's not about who did it first, it should all be done to glorify God. It's like our focus has abandoned our purpose. It's not about God anymore. It's about self-gratification. We get so caught up in the propaganda of things and people calling our names. Why? Pleasing ourselves should never be the motivating force of our lives.

We were created to please God, not ourselves, according to 1 Corinthians 10:31. Critical pleasure comes as a result of victimizing our flesh and vacating ourselves to the higher purposes of God as explained in Luke 9:23. Standing on God's Word and with God's Spirit makes us quicker to identify when our craving for self-gratification comes into struggle with what the Lord desires (Galatians 5:16–25).

We must take time to pray and ask God to lead us in the direction we should go. Ask Him to order our steps daily. I believe one of the greatest fears we have as women is not trusting one another. We are afraid of
being hurt.

We know that pain oh so well. We grew up hearing Aunt Becky saying, "don't trust that homewrecker!" So, we don't want people to get too close to us. We don't want to share ideas because we feel like someone is going to steal our ideas or do it first. Society has labeled black women in particular as 'difficult'. They say, "They are nothing but drama, loud, or trouble!" Some women are afraid to be a part of something great. They are afraid of getting hurt or fears confrontations. Among any group of people, problems can arise.

Having effective communication is extremely important. We must be willing to listen not just listen to respond. When we have a disagreement with our spouse, do we break up? No, we find ways to work it out. As women, why can't we do the same? No, we go and start creating posts about them. We start a blocking spree. We start patronizing their character. Instead of saying, "Sis, that hurt me." I can almost bet that it was only a simple misunderstanding. We tend to hear what we want to hear. How many people are still mad with a friend from high school? Do you remember what the argument was about? We are still holding on to feelings over things that you cannot even remember in full detail. We say, "I cannot stand her!" But, why? "Girl, it's just something about her!" Well, maybe we see something in her that we don't see in ourselves. Or better yet, go to God and pray for that sister!

Maybe, she's going through something personal. Women go through real life issues. As women, we struggle with infertility, higher rates of poverty, under-compensation, domestic violence, low self-esteem, and victim blaming, just to name a few. Most haven't shared their personal struggles with a soul. Depression and suicide are real!

What we say can make or break a person. Let's use our words to edify and for helping our sisters. Let's stop being so inclusive and reach out to the ones who are being left out. Do not allow the Spirit of Offense to set in. I am not saying to allow toxic people into your life, but just love people for who they are. Show some empathy and compassion for one another. If we are the smartest person in our circle, we are in the wrong circle. We should always be teachable and ready to learn. If we see a sister hurting or in need, we must create an opportunity for her, if we are able. Let's use our resources. After we have helped her, do not go tell the world what you have done. Don't tag her in a post saying, "Look at me I'm a good person, see!" Simply, continue to pray for her, because all the glory goes to our Dear Heavenly Father.

Also, it is important to check ourselves. We aren't always right. Our intentions can be good, but sometimes we hurt others. It's ok to say, "I messed up." Self-evaluation is something we need to do often.

Self-evaluation is the way a person views him/herself. It is the constant process of defining personal growth and progress. We must look at our development, progress, and learn to determine what has improved, and what areas still need improvement. We all have room for improvement. I have been guilty
on so many occasions of using this term "I am real."
Well, if we are so real, it should be easy for us to own our mistakes.
I saved this paragraph for last on purpose. Because as women, we tend to care for ourselves last. It is important to take care of ourselves first. We must make ourselves a priority. We cannot be as effective, if we aren't caring for self. We genuinely have a heart to help others. It's a natural instinct. But are we really healthy? Are we really taking the time we need to heal ourselves? Are we hiding our own problem in the need to care for others? Are we in codependent relationships? Are we afraid to pursue our own dreams but constantly make others' dreams come true? Remember iron sharpens iron. Proverbs 27:17 says, "Iron sharpens iron, and one man sharpens another."

When iron blades are rubbed together, each becomes sharper and thus more effective. Likewise, when believers are involved in one another's lives, mutual edification occurs. We must grow together because we are better together.

CHAPTER 25
Women Helping Women
Star Word

Ephesians 2:10 KJV
"For we are workmanship, created in Christ Jesus unto good works, which God hath before ordained that we should walk in them."

It was the first time I have been on a plane in years. Here I go. I braced my heels tightly to the floor of the plane under my feet. I was on my way from Nashville, Tennessee to Dallas, Texas to attend a large Business Conference. There were no friends, business associates, or family attending the conference with me. This part of my journey in life was just for me. You see, my husband and I agreed that I would stay home for five years, until my youngest child was entering Kindergarten. Once he started school, I would be free to get back on the entrepreneur highway.

I had an event planning business and New York style Ultra Lounge event venue in Cedar Rapids, Iowa prior to learning that we were expecting in 2014. Due to sickness during the pregnancy, I had to close the venue. Shortly after our youngest was born, my husband who is from Tennessee wanted to return home. I agreed with the decision and we went to his home state to be nearer to his side of the family. We stayed with his parents until we could afford our own place, then moved to a town about 30 minutes away. Each of us secured jobs. I found work with a small business that focused on the needs of the elderly population that were living in their homes but had some challenges with daily task due to old age, health, or lack of family assistance. It was my job to schedule support staff with clients in a particular region or geographic area of Tennessee.

The job was stressful. I worked in an office with women that seemed to be miserable in their personal lives and brought that drama to work and poisoned the environment with negativity on a daily basis. Each day it was becoming more and more unbearable, the way staff was treated and the "I've been here longer than you," snootiness wasn't my cup of tea. I believe in empowerment. I had worked as a Domestic Violence Advocate for years prior to moving away from Iowa. The red flags about abusive tactics and behaviours being used in the office setting were popping up consistently. It was causing me to experience a great deal of anxiety.

One morning while at my desk listening to online steaming a woman came across the internet talking about her upcoming business conference (EpicCon17) that was going to be held in Dallas, in the Spring of 2017. I recall a strong urge to write on a piece of paper the name of the conference (which I kept) and that I would be attending. I sort of thought that was bizarre, because I had only been listening and following the Business Coach for a short period of time. I think I joined her Facebook group *Coach, Speak, & Serve,* a couple of weeks before I made the decision to go to the conference.

The woman's name is Aprille Franks also known as Epic Aprille to her thousands of followers on Facebook, Insta Gram, and Twitter. She calls herself a Master Business Coach. What really grabbed my attention was that she seemed to be successful as a female African-American entrepreneur that dropped out of high school, had a baby as a teen, and she came across as a no nonsense woman "doing the dang thang" in this digital space called the world-wide web! Aprille impressed me with her level of knowledge about business, technology, and how to make money on-line by Coaching and off-line by hosting live events and Master Classes.

There are some big names in coaching, speaking, writing, and television that I was aware of like Less Brown, Lisa Nichols, Iyanla Vanzant, Tony Robbins, and of course Oprah! But to connect with someone that was reachable in real time suddenly felt like an amazing possibility. I remember thinking, "Wow! This was what I had been doing with the women I was advocating on behalf of at the Court House, in the hospitals, and during our one-on-one peer counselling sessions."

By the time I turned thirty I became internally and spiritually aware that my life had greater purpose than what those dreadful twenties looked like. Can I get an Amen somebody?!

I had been detached from entrepreneurship for about five years prior to connecting with Aprille's brand. When I felt that push to write down that I would be attending her conference that year, I was also led to start a GoFundMe campaign. Seeking support online isn't anything I had ever thought I would do. Surprisingly people helped me, and I made it to the conference. I will share more about that later.

I had started to do live talks about six months prior to following Aprille on Facebook. My first conversations were called "Saturday sessions with Star." I spoke about leadership and always touched on the spiritual principles I believe in. I will never forget the first "live," which was an announcement regarding the upcoming date for my very first Saturday Session. My hands and legs were trembling because I was so consumed with fear about what people would think of me going "live."

As time went on it got easier to show up with confidence and share good content. It helped when people would participate by asking questions or sharing their thoughts.

I eventually resigned from my position as a scheduler, because I desired to feel what freedom from the negativity felt like again. I attended that big conference in Dallas before I left that job.

The day we landed in Dallas, the weather was wonderful, and I looked for my shuttle to transport me to the Hilton Hotel where the conference was being hosted.

I had connected online with a couple different Women that are also members of the Facebook group *Coach, Speak & Serve* and were planning to attend the conference too. Each of the women graciously allowed me to room with them on different nights of the conference in order to stay within my already tight budget for the weekend. The lobby was upbeat and busy but still comfortable. There was a beautiful lounge area across from the registration desk with several televisions mounted beside white walls that were designed with deep billowing waves like the white waves of an ocean meeting the sands edge. Other spaces were separated by huge sheets of thick glass walls lit with blue lights bringing an ultra-sleek and modern vibe. The lobby seating areas were decorated with several crushed velvet grey and white lounge sofas and chairs. There were gigantic planters spread throughout the lobby with trees that reached to the second floor.

I took the opportunity to relax, breath and let it settle in, that I was there at the Epic Conference. I was a little nervous, and excited all at the same time. I went "live," a couple of times to show my viewers and supporters that I had made it safely. I was waiting for my roommate to get there in order to check in to the room. While I was relaxing, I got hungry. I had the GoFundMe assistance, but I needed to use it very wisely if it was going to last until the end of my trip. The Hotel restaurant was costly in comparison to the budget I had for the trip.

The hotel offered rides to nearby stores and malls, so I took a ride to get a few items from the nearest Wal-Mart. My roommate on the first night had finally made it to the hotel as the evening glided into view. She was a beautiful black slender woman with kinky twist in her hair and she had such a sweet demeanor.

The next morning as I exited the elevator, what energy was present! People where everywhere, in the line for coffee at the small cafe, lined up to be seated at the restaurant, and checking in at the long tables down the hall where the doors to enter the conference was being held. Many of the attendees stood around talking and introducing ourselves.

The call from the staff to line up and prepare to enter the conference had come and the energy got even greater! I remember hearing music behind the doors in the room, and as soon as they opened the doors and I stepped into that room, people were dancing, clapping, giving high fives, and embracing each other with hugs. It was one of the proudest moments I have shared with a group of women outside of a prayer circle that I have ever experienced. The Epic Conference was filled with an abundance of information for new or seasoned persons on an entrepreneurial journey. That weekend brought me an abundance of new connections.

When I made it back home after the conference my online life took off. People where seeking collaborative connections and inviting me to speak on their platforms, in webinars, and on their on-line radio shows. Since the conference I have led two book projects and I am currently working on my third personal anthology project. I have gained coaching clients and a much broader audience than I would have ever sought to have had I not connected with so many different people at Epic.

Believe me I am only in the beginning stages of where God is going to take me in my journey of empowering women to live in their purpose. God has shown me a path that leads me towards every divine connection that he desires me to connect with. I plan to continue showing up in this space, walking along my purpose path. Take it from me, a girl from the mean Chicago streets; if I can move from the back of the line to the front of the line, you can too!

CHAPTER 26
Extraordinary Sisters
Leana Brackens Jefferson

Be encouraged when life frowns on you, know that "Greater is He that is within you, is greater than he that is in the world." I write this letter to you my *Extraordinary Sister*, first and foremost to let you to know, I see you. So, as I proceed on a journey of encouragement to you, know that God is always in the mist of each and everything. Know that being *Extraordinary* is simply how you were born; you are meant to be this way.

Know that you are uncommon, so never let anyone treat you common. Understand that you can sound confident and have anxiety. You can look healthy, but your inside is falling apart. You can be as pretty as a super model on the outside and feel unapologetically ugly on the inside, remember that this life is filled with many battles and scares, but also know that you are not alone, you are my sister.

Remember that one must never pursue the spiritual disciplines as an end unto themselves. Instead pursue a closer relationship with God through the practice and power of the Holy Spirit (Edwards, 2013). In other words, rely on "means of grace" that which the Holy Spirit uses to conform us more and more to the image of our Lord and Savior Jesus Christ. *"Neither height nor depth, nor anything else in all creation, will be able to separate us from the love of God that is in Christ Jesus our Lord."* (Rom. 8:39 NIV).

My sister use your God ordain practices in your walk and hold your head up high, because you are walking with an anointing that has the favor of the King. This is how you grow and flow in His mercies and grace. Let no man speak ill of you, just because he or she cannot understand your anointing. This is God ordained. I encourage you to practice biblical spiritual disciplines daily. Know that this is a means to the transformation of your character.

There will be times when one must change their environment and or circle. When your circle gets smaller, know that your vision has gotten bigger. Love yourself, because life has a way of making one think that you must be great for people, when this should be the last means of a contenting life.

Be kind to yourself and know that God will never leave you. You, that's who, my sister reading this letter you are great and worthy of all that God has in store for you, so receive it and glow. Move your beautiful feet and walk boldly. Start to commune with God though practices of spiritual disciplines, such as scripture mediation, memorization, prayer, fasting, solitude and worship.

Scripture mediation and memorization are essential to your growth. Learn to rely on the amazing strength of God. Promise yourself that you will always remember just how amazing you are as well; you are His child. You are strong, bright, intelligent, and brave, you are *Extraordinary*. You are stronger than you think or ever give yourself credit for and braver than people think. Know that you have what it takes, you are your strongest weapon, use it my sister!

Dream about your future and go after it with Gods blessings. You need to see your scars in a new and beautiful light, use them to your advantage. Scars are a reminder of what you've been through, which means you have already made it out, so what God lifts out of you no man can thrust down.

Set goals and accomplish them, this is your road to becoming everything God has created you to be. Look for God's goodness, God is desiring to be good to those who are looking for His goodness. Read and continue to mediate on the word of God, knowing that His word is true. Mediation is a purgative of the mind and purification to your spirit. This is your special time to commune with the Father. Let him come into your space and feel the refreshing and newness of the Spirit. There is no wrong guidance in His word.

My sister in this life everyone at one time or another has been hurt and scared. You cannot live life without them, but the good news is what will you do or how will you respond? God said, *"And if anyone wants to sue you and take your shirt, hand over your coat as well"* (Matthew 5:40 NIV). Know who you are and who's you are.

Be ready, steadfast and unmovable in your journey. Hold fast to His commands and lead with a pure and loving heart. God knows what you need. Step out on faith and move those beautiful feet and walk boldly. You're an *Extraordinary Sister*.

Prayer, fasting and solitude feeds our faith. So, you prayed, and you believed, but what you ask God for has not yet come to pass. That in which we sometimes cannot see in the moment, but through prayer, fasting and solitude in the unseen realm was cut off, God was fulfilling your request.

God says, *"I will break the strength of the wicked, but I will increase the power of the Godly*. (Psalm 75: 10 NLT). You must hold fast to what God has placed in your spirit. If you want to know what your life will look like a year from now, listen to what you are feeding your spirit about yourself today. Your words are seeds planted in your soul; they are the harvest in your future. Be careful what you plant. Ask yourself what would happen if you trusted God with the future that He entrusted to you? Look no further; yesterday is the past, tomorrow is a mystery and today you are living in His presence.

You have the authority, but you do not have the respect, because you have not claimed it. Whenever you are in His presence and the flow stops, keep moving anyway. It will be what God has set out for it to be, so, decree and declare it. Speak over yourself, because your "next" is waiting. I'm coming straight through, in Jesus name!

Remember the enemy is not interested in where you are, it's where you're going; have stubborn faith!

The bible says, *"for a righteous man may fall seven times and rise again, but the wicked shall fall by calamity."* (Proverbs 24:16 NKJV). Stop letting people tell you what you cannot do. Do not let their story become your story. Never let what others think about you become more important then what God thinks about you. His plans are good and not of evil. His plans are greater than yours. He is not in the business of meeting your expectations but exceeding them.

Hallelujah!! For I know the plans I have for you," declares the LORD, "plans to prosper you and not to harm you, plans to give you hope and a future (Jeremiah 29:11 NIV). God still has a tomorrow for your today. Faith is your test of your dependence of your trust in God. My sister…move your beautiful feet and walk boldly, you are *Extraordinary*. Now, worship in reverent honor of God. Praise your way into the celebration of a lifetime. Do not be a hoarder in your mind, clear out all the clutter. God is your vindicator.

He has already set the table in the presence of your enemies. My sister; keep your mind stayed on Him. Everything you have been through has prepared you for now. This is your finest hour and this moment is your greatest opportunity to step out of the shadows of mediocrity and into the

realm of greatness. You are fearless and courageous. Claim what God had rightfully given you, it's yours. God has entrusted you with His reputation. He has instilled gifts in you for others to enjoy and celebrate with you. Be kind in your works, be humble, obedient and submissive in your servitude. Your true impartation will show. God will guide you into your "next."

True humility helps us to follow the one who is the founder and perfecter of our faith. Remember what God has entrusted in you is too big for you to be small. God will not withhold any good thing. Be grateful for the resource but keep your eyes on the source. Seek the wisdom

of the Holy Spirit. Please… my sister, do not be casual with God's word. Seek the Lord for your next assignment.

The joy of the Lord is your strength. Also, discernment should be one of your greatest friends in your worship and season of your Next. Pray that you see but do not be shaken by what you discover, because some things that will be uncovered in 2020 may shake your feelings but will not shake your faith. God is in this, live life forward and you will learn from it backwards.

God sees you not just as a contender but as a Champion and Child of the Most-High. I leave you with this, my sister; some people can only celebrate you at their level of comprehension. You have a different authority on you. Now, write it down and make it plain. Regardless of the grade you received, don't throw away the notes. God doesn't have an adversary. So, believe and receive all that God has for you, and move your beautiful feet and walk boldly. Your "next" is waiting, because you are an *Extraordinary Sister*!

CHAPTER 27
The Overcomer
LaKesha Perdue

Proverbs 3:5-6
"Trust in the Lord with all thine heart and lean not to thy own understanding. In all thine ways acknowledge him, and he shall direct thy paths."

Hey girl! Yes you! I want you to know that you too can make it. Pick your head up and know that you were built for this. How do I know? I am glad that you asked. I'm an overcomer. I am more than what you thought of me. I am more than what momma and others thought I would be and way more than what the enemy was telling me that I was. I survived being a mother at the age of eighteen. Eighteen? Yes, me! Some look at me and say there is no way you have three adult children. Well it didn't start off this way.

I had to do an early out program in high school because I was lacking attention of something or someone. I had hidden in my heart the pain, shame and guilt of being molested, by not just one of my mother's brothers, but also from one of her sisters. I didn't know how to deal with the situation, so I began fighting, getting suspended from school and even being jailed at seventeen with my cheerleading uniform on. Imagine that! I recall telling the one who was supposed to protect me from all the big bad wolves in the world until I was able to protect myself.

You see this began when I was only ten years old. My aunt and her then husband who was more like family before he legally became family moved in after getting married. It all worked for my single over-night working mother. Hey, she could go to work and not worry about her kids being home alone; although we were old enough to stay by ourselves. My aunt began to sexually assault me in ways I didn't know. She began having me do things to her that I only seen on T.V. after a certain time of the night. You know when you snuck and watched HBO, and Cinemax because it's what we all laughed and talked about at school as children. Yeah, we knew we shouldn't, but we'd hear our families watching these channels and couldn't wait to have a moment when no adults were around to find out what it was. We wondered what they were watching. I know, I know.

As the enemy had it planned and sat up to destroy my mind at an early age, he used my aunt to taunt me and manipulate me into doing things all at the cost of being able to watch my favorite musician Michael Jackson. She knew I'd do whatever in order to watch him after mom had gone to work.

I never told my mother of this abuse, the fear of hurting her feelings and knowing that she'd blame herself for allowing them to come stay in our home. My mother was a God-fearing woman until the day she passed. I've seen my mother fighting about her kids. I've seen and heard her cuss folks and teachers out about her kids. But this, would have taken her all the way out! I was able to get past this time in my life with the help of the Lord at an early age. I cried out to God asking him why he'd allow such things to happen to a child. I didn't really know Gods voice then, so I began coloring and picked up an interest in arts. I would spend hours in my room coloring, I would always do anything to try and keep my younger two siblings near me or in eye view. Even at that time, I was on track to be an overcomer of the plans of the enemy. Nevertheless, I asked God why me? Why me? God said, "Child I have you in the palm of my hands and you are not damaged goods. You don't understand the purpose behind the pain, but there is purpose."

Listen lady, you can make it through! You *must* make it through. You're still alive; scars and all. God has a plan for you. Its working for your good!

I went through another couple years of toxic relationships to try to drown out the cries of the shame and confusion I felt in my life. I was taking part in things that I knew I should not be involved with. I moved to Detroit, Michigan on a mission of being "grown." I started drinking and becoming promiscuous.

I became with child again, but I was not ready for motherhood again. I cried and begged God to take this child from me because I didn't want to face having another child so soon. I don't believe in abortion so that was not an option, although my friends were trying to convince me to do so. I had to do something. I took several pills trying to destroy this fetus that was not going to make its way through me. A few hours had passed and then a day or so. I became very ill. I had chills, fever, nausea and cold sweats. I began to cramp so bad that I'd get in the passenger seat and ball myself up. What gave me the right to destroy a life? I had so many questions and concerns about what was going on in my life. I lost that baby and while going through those events. I almost killed myself.

I found myself in Hutzel Hospital in Detroit, Michigan. I remember lying there on that cold table as the physician told me they had to pump my stomach to get the pills out of my system. My body was ridding itself of a fetus and fighting overdose levels of medication in my body. But God spared my life once again. He said, "no matter what you try to do, I still love you and it'll be for my glory." I laid in the bed and wept. I called my mother and family. I was there by myself without family with me. God said, "but I have need of you and it's time to go back home." I didn't fight it, but neither did I move upon his direction either.

Shortly after recovering from that ordeal, my dad took ill and my sister told me the doctors gave him a couple of months to live. I remember getting drunk that night because I felt like I just couldn't take life anymore! God had to use my dad to get ill for me to return home. A few months later dad passed.

I started going back to church and I reconnected with a childhood friend and we began dating off and on for a year. Then we finally got serious enough to "claim" our relationship as "us." We dated for another year and then it happened...I'm with child. No, I wasn't proud of what I had done but I thought "she's here now and I'm in love all over again." Seven months after her birth we were married. I never told anyone not even myself that this is what God had planned for us. We just felt like we loved each other, and we started a family. He wanted to be in ministry and the church wasn't having it any other way.

Ahh! The bliss of marriage. I remember telling myself, "Everything should be gravy from here." Well, we knew that wasn't real life.

It all began a few years into the marriage. That's when the cheating started. The habitual name calling, and the disrespect was tossed around like a wet dirty rag. I will never blame it all on him, but for the most part it was because of his actions. We overcame that first run of trials and it was years later that I found myself with child again. He was continually unfaithful, and the marriage took on another trial.

We had meetings with the pastor, and our marriage seemed to work for a few more years; or he was very clever about it. Either way, I had been dropped once again! I remember telling God, "okay, this is it!I cannot take this anymore." My initial response was to fight. It's what I knew to do. It's what I *wanted* to do. I was not only hurt by him but also the people we called friends. How could this be happening? God said he'll never put more on us than we can bare, and He made away for escape.

I went through health issues to the point that I was planning my own funeral. I recall asking my ex-husband who he'd be with because I needed to know who my children were going to be around. God had to remind me that I was an overcomer, and to pick myself up and heal. I had to literally move away from where I was living for God to heal me completely. This was not an easy task. I was reminded of the story of Job and how he lost everything! His friends called him crazy. They couldn't understand how Job could lose everything and still serve God. I was in that same situation.

My family couldn't understand how I had to leave my familiar place and relocate to uncommon grounds. This is the place where healing had to take place.

I thought I was losing my mind on so many occasions that I was ready to check my own self into a facility. I called out to God to remind Him of His words to me. All I kept hearing was "YOU ARE AN OVERCOMER." I didn't want to hear that. I wanted the solution. I wanted my children! I wanted to lay in my mother's bed in a ball and cry it out! I wanted to hurt those who hurt me! But I had to trust God in everything.

God will not put more on you than you are able to bear. You think you can't take it? You think you can't walk away from that abusive relationship? You think that God is not with you? I am declaring that God is with you! I am a living witness that if you just call out to Him, He will make away of escape for you. You are an overcomer!

I regained everything that I lost and more. My health is in pretty good condition. I have a good relationship with all my children and, I am now an entrepreneur of four streams of income. I speak to women of all ages to let them know that they too can be an overcomer. I had to trust God! I want you to know that there is a place in God for you. You were created with purpose; no matter how you get there. You will love again. You will become successful. You will regain what you may have lost and so much more. You must trust and believe in your purpose. You must know that you are beautifully and wonderfully made in the image of God. We need to take responsibility for our actions that may have caused us to take some of the difficult paths that we have taken, but we are overcomers. Lady, you have so much value within you that the world is waiting on. I know you can do it! You are smart, you are beautiful, you are valuable, you are loved, and you are needed. You are more than the negative words spoken over you from that broken person who had not previously been healed. Woman know your worth and get busy living as an overcomer! I pray that you know that you are not alone. You are not the only one. You can become the overcomer within you that's screaming to come out. Many blessings to you my sister, my new friend...the overcomer!

My prayer is that you are freed from the strong grips of your past and even your present. I pray that you allow God to heal completely and straighten your crown. Walk with your head held high and put a smile on your face. Let the sparkle in your eyes return and you will live as the overcomer that you are.

Blessings,
LaKesha Perdue

Scripture References:
KJV 1 Peter 4:12:13, Revelations 12:11

CHAPTER 28
Seize the Moment
Erica Jackson

Blackness. Silence. Time stood still and I felt like I was in a room with no way to escape. I tried screaming for help, but I couldn't even open my mouth. I tried to run but my legs were like stone.
What is happening? Am I dreaming? Suddenly I saw a small light and heard muffled voices. My eyes opened slowly, and I saw people standing over me. "Are you okay baby girl?" I heard a lady ask me. She looked familiar but I just couldn't remember who she was. I barely remembered who I was or where I was for that matter. I assumed I looked confused because the woman asked me if I remembered who she was. I slowly shook my head.
"What happened?" I finally asked. "You passed out and started shaking." the woman replied. And before I knew it, I was getting rushed to the ER.
I didn't understand what was happening and why my body felt weird. I didn't have control of my own body and I needed to be in control. I panicked and blacked out.

When I came back, I woke up in a room that was filled with beeping monitors and people staring. I was still confused. I saw that woman again looking at me while smiling. My memory was slowly coming back and I realized that woman was my mother. How could I forget who my own mother was? What was happening? A few days later, at the age of 13, I was diagnosed with Epilepsy.

I went through junior high, high school and even college battling with seizures. I had seizures weekly and this put my body and brain through so much. My memory suffered as well as my self-esteem and my will to live. I isolated myself from friends and family, tried many times to kill myself, had no appetite which caused me to lose so much weight that I weighed 90 pounds by the age of 14.

I found myself in a deep depression that was hard to get out of. I had to be home bound my junior year and a portion of my senior year of high school. I was told by my doctor that high school and college would be a struggle for me because my comprehension skills were not the same as they were before the diagnosis of epilepsy, due to some damage within my brain. My mother looked the doctor in the eye and said, "You don't know the God I serve."
We walked out of the doctor's office determined to prove that we serve a powerful God, and this *will not* be a test, but it will be a true testimony.

As time went on, my faith was getting weak. I began to get impatient with God. That impatience turned into anger and that get became rage. I blamed God for cursing me with seizures. I would go to church and not even acknowledge God. I didn't even have a praise because why praise a God that claims He loves you, yet He allows bad things happen to you? I wanted nothing to do with God. I questioned Him time and time again wanting to know why this had to happen to me. I felt that it was because of Him cursing me that I could no longer praise dance anymore because too much movement triggered my seizures. It was because of Him that my body had bruises and damaged nerves due to the fact that my seizures were so severe. I often asked myself, "Why should I thank Him?"

Just when I was getting back on track, my grandmother passed away. I went right back into the depression I was in and became even more angry with God. He had already cursed me once and then He took away my rock? I was done with God at that point. I was very angry with Him for making my life a living hell. My anger was only soothed by secretly cutting myself. The relief I felt when doing it was what I needed to escape my troubles. After a while, cutting myself wasn't helping me anymore. I needed another escape from my life. The only option I had left was to kill myself.

I planned everything out and was ready to execute my plan until I heard a voice say "Jeremiah 29:11-14" I found a Bible in my closet and went to the scripture that read:

"For I know the thoughts that I think toward you, saith the Lord, thoughts of peace, and not of evil, to give you an expected end. Then shall ye call upon me, and ye shall go and pray unto me, and I will hearken unto you. And ye shall seek me, and find me, when ye shall search for me with all your heart. And I will be found of you, saith the Lord: and I will turn away your captivity, and I will gather you from all the nations, and from all the places whither I have driven you, saith the Lord; and I will bring you again into the place whence I caused you to be carried away captive."

I immediately went into tears and found myself pouring out my heart to God. I repented for me blaming Him. I told Him if this is His will then it shall be done. He gave me an assignment, but I would have to trust Him and believe He is able. I told Him I was a vessel and I will do whatever it takes to fulfill my assignment. Once I gave my life back to Him, I knew my life would never be the same.

I walked across the stage at my high school graduation with a heart full of gratitude and a praise. After graduating high school, I knew I wanted to go to college. I knew that I would have to work even harder because of my comprehensive skills and also my focus skills weren't like others. But I knew with God on my side, I would walk across that stage to receive my degree.

I was excited when I got accepted to college but that was short lived when my stepdad told me college is a waste of time and I am grown enough to get a job. He said that I wouldn't succeed if I went to college. He told his preacher friends I was trying to go to college.

One of his friends "prophetically" claimed that I would get pregnant first year and drop out. He talked down to me, but I was accustomed to that since things had gotten bad between us years prior. He was always against me and jealous of the relationship I had with my mother. He verbally abused my siblings, my mother and I constantly. He even took his tactics to the pulpit. He blamed me for his failing marriage to my mother rather than taking responsibility for his own actions. He spoke so much negativity and caused a lot of grief in my life.

I was determined to prove him wrong. I went to college anyways and he made it his business to discourage me each time he had a chance but acted like he loved me in public. Once he found out he didn't have control of my faith and that I was still in college, his tactics got worse. He would twist stories about me to make me seem like I was a bad child. People were really believing him, and they would try to scold me. I was so confused but I knew he was upset that I was doing so well in college and wanted me to be knocked off my path.

Once he and my mother got divorced, the dark cloud that hovered over my family went away. We were happy again and I was even more determined to be an example to my siblings and make my mother proud. Although I was still battling seizures in college, I didn't give up. I kept my faith. I stood tall in my purpose and walked like a giant into my destiny. I made it my priority to advocate for Epilepsy Awareness on my college campus but in my community as well.

I was excelling on my campus, I was in honor societies, many clubs and organizations. I didn't let seizures, or my social anxiety get to me. Even though I was doing well in college, I wanted to live a little on the wild side. I began partying more and drinking and hanging with people I had no business being around. I found myself back in a depression once again. I knew this wasn't the life God had for me. I was letting Him down and letting myself down as well.

I got a hold of myself and prayed that God would guide my footsteps and help keep me on the right path. After that, I excelled again and became campus royalty and president of other clubs. I was happy once again. I was myself again.

As soon as I got back on track, I had an intense seizure at home that had me close to death. My little brother and mother had to perform CPR until the ambulance came. At the hospital, I cried but this time it wasn't because I was upset about me having a seizure, I was thanking God for sparing me. I was on bed rest for days because of the damage the seizure did to my body.

I didn't complain, instead I worshipped the whole time until I was well enough to go back to class. I dived into my work and kept my focus on the goal; to graduate.

May 14th of 2017, I walked across that stage with gratitude in my heart once again and a praise but unlike last time, this praise couldn't be contained any longer. I felt a praise in my feet and before I knew it, I was shouting soon as I got off the stage. I gave God my best praise and I did not care who saw. I endured so much those 4 years that it was truly a blessing I made it to this place in my life. No matter what the enemy may throw at you, when you are God's child, you will dodge every attack!!

I'm doing well now. I am in my career and I am currently working on my master's degree. I get discouraged every now and then, but I always remember that each day is a gift from God. I didn't let seizures stop me from living.

Don't you let anything, or anyone stop you! We are God's daughters and He wants to see us prosper and be the Queens we are! The enemy wants us to give up. The enemy wants us to forfeit our assignment and doubt God. DO NOT fall for his tricks! We are powerful women! When we wake up and place our feet on the floor, satan trembles! Wake up each morning my Queens, put on your crown and seize the moment! Seize each moment with love, joy, peace and gratitude! Seize the moment!

CHAPTER 29
The Price of Peace and Sanity Choose You
Mikayla Thompson

Have you or someone you know ever experienced heartbreak? Have you ever wondered why some women find love and others it seems as though they have to go through all the sons of pharaoh before they find their one true love? There is a plethora of women that can say they have been through hell and high waters before they met their true love. Most even tend to ask "what is wrong with me? Why won't a good man ever pick me? What signs do I need to look out for?" We may simply wonder why we didn't see the signs. Let's dive deeper into that subject.

The typical image that pops into most people's head after hearing the word narcissist, is an overly confident individual who shares characteristics of an extreme extrovert. What some women miss, is that they may have dated a narcissist and not even realized it.

There are levels and categories to narcissism. The first type that is the most commonly thought of is an exhibitionist narcissist. These are the kind of individuals that thrive off of admiration and attention. They typically lack empathy and expect perfection from others. Their inflated ego causes them to overlook any flaws they have and will refuse to acknowledge any mistake that they make. They have a relationship style that requires their significant other to agree with absolutely everything they chose to say or do and a difference in opinion is recognized as a challenge or scrutiny.

Underneath those narcissists are the individuals that obsess over them and find self-worth by simply being associated with them. Those individuals are labeled as closet narcissists. This could be observed in a cliché high school movie where the mean guy crew has that one quiet guy that is not truly like the ringleader. He is quiet but has found a way to attach himself to someone to feel special. In relationships they are typically emotionally destructive and have devised a victim mentality. No amount of coddling, consideration, or reassurance will fulfill their needs or execute their feeling of emptiness. These are the kinds of people that you would end up feeling sorry for and start demoralizing yourself. DO NOT DO IT. This is equally as exhausting as being in a relationship with an exhibitionist narcissist.

The third narcissist is categorized as the toxic narcissist. Toxic narcissists don't seek gratification from being the center of attention or attaching themselves to someone who is the center of attention.

These are the individuals that obsess on stealing joy from people and establishing dominance through fear and seek challenges from people even though they haven't initiated one. Their primary goal in a relationship is to make you feel inferior and constantly verbally abuse you. They expect all of the praise and give none.

Sometimes it can be hard to pinpoint a narcissist because all these characteristics are embedded into the personality and it doesn't always present itself. If you recognize ANY of these red flags it is important to nip it in the bud early so that it won't be difficult to remove yourself from the situation. If a relationship costs you your peace or sanity, it is not worth it.

Now, not every man is a narcissist, but you learned a great deal of things just reading about the characteristics of one, didn't you? There are other toxic traits that you should be aware of when dating men. Even though they aren't clinically labeled, there still could be red flags to watch out for. What is the most common complaint of women when dating a guy that they're unsure of? Have you ever found yourself saying, "why doesn't he answer his phone?" If you have ever asked this question, then that means you are paying attention to his communication style and habits.

Initiating communication is a key factor in recognizing how a man feels about you. If he does not typically answer within a reasonable time frame, he either finds his other priorities more important than you, doesn't obligate you as one of those priorities or...well that is just it. If a man truly desires you, you will not have to fight tooth and nail for his attention. He will make his intentions clear about being with you in fear of losing you. It's a painful truth but once you accept it, you will thank yourself for cutting ties.

The second most common issue is cheating. Let's be real for a second, not all men cheat and not all men cheat for the same reasons. However, that does not dismiss the fault. Some men cheat out of pure unfettered impulse. Others may cheat simply out of selfishness. Regardless of the matter it's important that you must first change the source of your perspective from emotional to psychological. The psychological stand of why men cheat whereas the emotional standpoint are two different sub regions.

If you change the "what" to "why", you can recognize the kind of man you are dealing with and you will obtain closure. Most women obsess over the fact that he cheated and hurt them emotionally. Some women move on and others end up being emotionally scarred for years. Psychologically speaking, when a man cheats, it's typically because it was an impulse derived from his needs. A needs-driven person hardly ever functions through their life on a foundation of principles. Their primary principle is to live by their own principle and that principle is to do what feels good and not what is good. A selfish streak like this is reckless because this type of man lacks the discipline to be sufficient in his own life let alone faithful to another person.

If you have ever been cheated on it is important to acknowledge the fact that he has some issues that he needs to resolve and some growing up to do on his own. It has absolutely ZERO to do with your capability to be a good woman. You are enough, you are beautiful, and it just so happened that you met a man who has not yet established discipline and moral reasoning as a basic principle in his life. That has nothing to do with you at all. He needs to figure that out on his own. It's not your job to teach that to him sis. He is a grown man so let him figure that out on his own. Until he realizes that and makes the change for himself, he won't make the change for anyone else. Let that man go so you can move forth and prosper with your own dreams and aspirations.

At the end of the day, it is important to trust yourself. Pay attention to your body spiritually, physically, and mentally when it comes to dating, decision making, or anything in life for that matter. Life is full of milestones that you experience step by step. If you ever feel lost, think about what you used to do in high school when you didn't understand the step by step math problems. What did you do? You sought tutoring and exhausted your resources.

Your body is a compass that can guide you better than anyone else you know. I advise you to value and care for yourself. Treasure your sanity and peace. Once you make that genuine connection with yourself you will inevitably stop excepting things for what they are or "could be". You will start to be leery about people or things that could disrupt the peace in your space. You will stop doing what others expect of you and stop satisfying everyone around you.

Lastly, I want you to know that just because you've been through what you've been through, that does not mean you are weak. And because you are hurting, it does not mean you are weak. It means you are human. You have feelings, and you've just been through something. Take a deep breath look at yourself in the mirror and be proud that you are still standing. The next step you take needs to be an intentional step of confidence and without apology. Then, connect with yourself on a positive and balanced level, you will achieve true happiness.

When women base their happiness in life on finding the right men, they tend to obsess over that man and demoralize themselves why? They fixate and glorify that man's every move, hang onto their every word and are infatuated. The questions that have not been answered in life yet, are the answers that you would look to him to give. You would end up basing your very existence on pleasing him and not being in a reciprocal relationship.

Some women end up demoralizing themselves by being content with the simple fact that they have a man, so they allow their actions to fly without consequences. The only man that deserves glory, praise, and that level of adoration is God.

Once you've preoccupied your mind with finding a man, that is when you have contradicted your belief system. This is typically why most women have not found love yet. God wouldn't send you a man that you would place above Him. You need to achieve that level of happiness and contentment with yourself first.

As far as a significant other, always remember that you are married in spirit before you are married in the flesh. If you continue to have the self-discipline to do what is best for you and establish solid morals and understanding of life, you will be less stressed. Your significant other will eventually gravitate towards you. Your worlds will instantly bond with one another seamlessly because both of you value your peace and refuse to risk it over someone that is unsure of you or themselves for that matter.

Above anything, do not make the main focus of your life "when will a good man pick me?" YOU pick you first. Know that you are enough with or without a man. Think about what makes an athlete a good athlete. They achieve discipline, self-trust, and balanced self-esteem. They first recognize that they're enough without the gold medal and they are enough with the gold medal. It is something short of a mental game. In simple terms, you need to recognize that you are enough with a man and you are enough without a man.

Remember …do not worry about when a man will pick you. You pick you first. YOU find the gem in you first and you will appreciate your significant other in the future for admiring the hard work you put towards yourself. You will beam confidence, grace, discipline, and peace from within and be thankful that it is because of you and not a man. Pick you first. Pick you.

CHAPTER 30
The Favor of God
Mary E. Carrethers

January 26, 1999 at 12:15 am, was a time that would forever change our lives. I was at work and received a telephone call telling me that I needed to come home because our house was on fire and our son did not make it out of the house. My supervisor drove me home, and on the way, I was trying to wrap my head around what was going on. I had left the house an hour earlier and watched our son go upstairs to bed.

Let me start from the day before. On Monday January 25, 1999, I awoke and felt very ill. All day long I could not shake the feeling that a tragedy was coming to our family, but I did not know who or why. I was told by the Spirit to hug our son Johnny and tell him everything was going to be okay. I told Johnny when he got home from school that everything was going to be okay, but I did not hug him as instructed and I regret it to this day.

I worked at night, so I slept in the daytime. While lying in bed I could smell smoke but when I got up to check it out, I could no longer smell anything. When I went upstairs the walls were carpeted and they felt hot but when I came downstairs and checked the walls felt normal.

At 10:30 pm my husband Joseph drove me to work but on my way to the car I turned and looked at the house because I felt as though I would never see it again. At 11:45 pm I called home to check on Johnny, but he did not answer.

Fast forward to arriving home at 12:45 am to fire trucks, ambulances, news crews, detectives, neighbors, and a husband telling me how sorry he was that he tried but could not save him. Joseph was trying to reach Johnny's bedroom window by ladder, and he was told that every time he went up the ladder he would fall back to the ground. Joseph does not remember falling and he was not hurt. We believe an Angel caught him every time he fell.

After they took Johnny's body away at 4 am, a feeling of helplessness and disbelief was all I could feel after all he was only 17 years old. Joseph and I climbed on the roof and went through the window to get into Johnny's bedroom. His TV was melted but he had money lying beside the TV and it was untouched. His shoes were melted to the floor, but his bed was untouched by the flames. There was a paper sack with candy and soda, but it too was untouched. At the head of the bed was a radio and recording equipment that was melted but again his bed was untouched. The ceiling, walls, and furniture were all burnt but his body was untouched. It was as though GOD had put a bubble around him and anything he had touched.

I never ask GOD why he allowed this to happen, but I did thank GOD for taking care of our son. I believe GOD was protecting his child from the evils of this world. Even though it has been 21 years, to me it was like yesterday. Isaiah 57:1-2 says *"The righteous perisheth, and no man layeth it to heart: and merciful men are taken away, none considering that the righteous is taken away from the evil to come. He shall enter into peace: they shall rest in their beds, each one walking in his uprightness."* Always listen to the Spirit. Trust GOD and He will take care of you.

Mary E. Carrethers

ABOUT THE AUTHOR

Evangelist Tanya R. Thompson
Founder & CEO
Glory After the Rain Ministries

Evangelist Tanya R. Thompson is an African American Christian Author. She is the mother of one daughter, Mikayla (Kayla) Thompson who is currently a Senior Interdisciplinary Studies major at Tennessee State University. Thompson became a Licensed Nurse in 2003. For the last nine years, she has worked as a Utilization Review Nurse for a large healthcare corporation located in Franklin, TN. She is the CEO and Founder of Glory After the Rain Ministries. Tanya presents a Facebook live Early Morning Devotional series on Facebook that attracts viewers from across the continent and other countries. In addition to this, she is pursuing a long-awaited dream of podcasting. Evangelist Tanya travels the country spreading the message of Jesus Christ through Women's Conferences, Revivals, Talk Shows and Workshops. She currently offers writing courses online for women who desire to birth their first book. She currently holds an Associate of Divinity degree and a Bachelor of Divinity degree from Christian Leaders Institute and Christian Leaders College in Grand Rapids, MI. She was ordained as a Deaconess and subsequently an ordained Minister through Pastor Henry Reyenga of Grand Rapids, Michigan. Tanya is currently pursuing a dual enrollment program to obtain her Master and Ph.D. in Theological studies. She also desires to become a Board-Certified Christian Counselor in the near future.

Evangelist Tanya is a contributing writer for *Faith Heart Magazine*. She has written a total of eight books: *After the Rain*, (2015) *Straight from the Heart – A 30 Day Devotional* (2018), *Redemption* (2019), *Silent Suffering* (2019), *Women Who Worship – A 30 Day Devotional* (2019), *He Loves Me Not* (2019), *Five Smooth Stones* (2020) *The Courageous Story of the Prophet Elijah* (2020)

Evangelist Tanya was featured in K.I.S.H. Magazine as one of the "Top 40 Most Influential Dreamers, Movers & Shakers" for 2020. Her true passion is the empowerment of women who have been affected by domestic violence. As a survivor of domestic violence, she is committed to speaking out and telling the story of those directly affected by this horrible epidemic. She has found a great satisfaction in bringing women of all walks of life together in unity. You can find Evangelist Tanya on Facebook live, where she hosts a show called *Early Morning Devotional*.

Contact Evangelist Tanya R. Thompson:
Email: gloryaftertherain@gmail.com
Facebook: Tanya Thompson
Instagram: Tanya Thompson
YouTube: Evangelist Tanya Thompson
Phone: 615-300-4312

ABOUT THE AUTHOR

Evangelist Sraya Fears

Evangelist Sraya Fears is an inspirational Author, Prophetic Psalmist, Christian Evangelist, and Soror of Theta Phi Sigma Christian Sorority, Inc. also known as the Pink Society. She is currently attending the Apostolic Institute of Higher Learning to attain her Master of Advanced Prophetic Studies and Science of Spiritual Pneumatics in Prophetic Arts.
Evangelist Fears has a unique prophetic mantle over her life; her passion for God and surrendered lifestyle have led to an anointing to exhort, encourage, and empower young girls and women to pray and cultivate their God-given potential in their personal, spiritual, and professional lives. Her deep passion for abandon, broken, and hurting young girls and women birthed a ministry.
She is the CEO and Founder of *Highly Blessed Is She Ministries*. The women's ministry was founded to help activate the call of God in young girls and women to be strong, confident women of God by building their self-esteem, self-worth, and loving themselves as God loves and sees them. With humility and generosity of spirit, Evangelist Fears is released to flow in the Holy Spirit, she leaves an impartation that inspires believers to walk in holiness and higher dimensions of God.

Contact Evangelist Sraya Fears at:
hisdivineangel97@gmail.com

ABOUT THE AUTHOR

Pam Ryans is an author, entrepreneur, life coach, philanthropist, and publisher. Pam holds a Bachelor's in Business Management & Marketing, a Masters of Counseling and Psychology, and is a Certified Life Coach. She is the Founder of 1 Vision Empowerment; publishing and networking. She is a best-selling author and producer of other best-selling authors who utilize her publishing expertise. Additionally, Ms. Ryans is founder of *The Daughter of Sarah* (caregiver support) and *Transform Your Mind with Pam Ryans* (text and YouTube ministry). She is also a certified life coach, helping individuals refocus on their passion and redefine their purpose after a major life shift.

Most proudly, Pam is the mother of four amazing young ladies and grandmother of four vibrant joys of her life.

Visit her at www.1visionempowerment.com.

ABOUT THE AUTHOR

La Tonya Day

La Tonya Day is a Christian Life Coach who graduated with a Bachelor's Degree in Business Management. She is the creator and owner of *Eve Restored*, giving the gift of hope to women through R.E.S.T: Restoration, Encouragement, Sharpening, and Teaching. She is the wife and helpmate of Elder Deron Day and the mother of two handsome, witty and creative boys.

Connect with La Tonya Day at:
Eve Restored, LLC
La Tonya Day, Christian Life Coach

ABOUT THE AUTHOR

Chaundra Nicole Gore

Chaundra Nicole Gore, MSL is a Radio talk show host on the *Encouraging Yourself* Show on All Nations Stellar Award-Winning Radio station, Host of Thursday Night at 8 with *LensOfFaith* LIVE on Facebook/YouTube, leadership strategist, destiny catalyst, international speaker, motivational coach, ghostwriter, Amazon bestselling author, the Founder and CEO of Lens of Faith Photography LLC, *Lens of Faith Speaks* and *Discovering You Motivational Coaching Program*. She is a disabled Army Veteran who has served over 19+ years in United States Army. She is also a sexual assault victim's advocate, Moderator for Cultivating Clarity in our Community for Domestic Violence, and a member Kappa Epsilon Psi Military Sorority Inc. She is an advocate for Service members as a member of The Association for United States Army, Brand Ambassador for: *We Are Women of Substance*, L.I.F.T (Ladies Intentionally Following Through), *Black Women Handling Business*, and *Unstoppable Black Women*. Chaundra authored her first book in January 2019 titled, *"I Am A Lens of Faith"*, after becoming a co-author on her first *anthology "We Are Women of Substance."* She is also a co-author in *"Lift, Launch, Lead"*, *"Unleashing the Roar"* and *"100 Words of Inspiration."* She wrote the foreword on "The *Healing Journey"* and *"My Storm, My Story."* Outside of her professional titles, she is also a wife, mother of a blended family, and a survivor of domestic violence and sexual abuse. Chaundra is a Military award recipient of the Meritorious Service Medal x 3, Army Commendation Medal x 5, Army Achievement Medal x 2, Certificate of Appreciation x 4, Certificate of Excellence x 2 and numerous plaques and coins of excellence for my dedicated service to the United States Army and Army Reserve. She is currently married to Kenneth D. Gore Jr. for 11 years and they have a blended family of seven children. Chaundra has a B.S. in Business Management and an MS in Leadership. She is a Doctoral Student at Grand Canyon University pursuing Organizational Leadership.

ABOUT THE AUTHOR

Vanessa Scott

Vanessa Scott is the Founder & CEO of *Women with Open Arms* (WWOA), a non-profit organization. By day, Scott is an Insurance Specialist for a Home Health Agency in Nashville, TN where she has served for more than 14 years. WWOA was established in 2014 under the then name of D.I.V.A.S. of Nashville. The organization is near and dear to her due to her own experience with domestic violence. Scott loves pouring into women to offer them hope, encouragement, and support during their difficult times. Scott believes "she is to someone else what she had hoped someone would have been to her." This has been nothing short of her inspiration.

Scott is also a published author of *"The Lost and Found: My Journey to Life"* where she details her struggle with low self-esteem and self-worth, to motivate and encourage others who think that their past has to dictate their future. Scott is a living proof that it doesn't. When Scott isn't working her full-time job, she can be found making sure needs are being met through *Women with Open Arms*. Scott enjoys and loves family time, engaging conversation and watching home improvement shows.

You can reach Vanessa Scott at:
Women with Open Arms
3935 Clarksville Pike, Nashville TN 37218
615-436-0995
info@thewwoa.org

ABOUT THE AUTHOR

Queen Glenda King

Queen Glenda Brown-King served in the U.S. Army for over 25 continuous yearsof service before retiring in 2017. She is a graduate of the Defense Information School, Fort Meade, MD and working towards completing her degree at Liberty University in VA. Queen Glenda started her career as a stenographer in the military and later became a career counselor, paralegal, human resources officer and journalist. She's served in various assignments to include, Operation Iraqi Freedom and Operation Enduring Freedom. She also worked as a Department of Defense Civilian as a public affairs and protocol specialist. Queen Glenda received one of her greatest fulfillments while working as a volunteer at her local church in the community outreach ministry. She worked to influence and inspire children and their families to choose paths in life that bring them to a higher place of accomplishment and change. She has served as secretary for the Association of the United States Army, Francis Scott Key Chapter, Ft. Meade, MD, Chaplain and secretary for the Retired Enlisted Association, Chapter 24, Ft. Meade, MD, a member of *Women Veterans Interactive*, Houston's *Dress for Success* and was named as an honoree for Houston's 2018 Black Excellence Pageant Awards for her service in community outreach. She is an entrepreneur and CEO of Community Outreach, *"Bringing Families Closer Together!"*, substitute teacher, member of the Catholic Charities Galveston Military Women's Group and Communications Specialist for the CEO, *Soar to the Top Training Center*, Severn, MD. Queen Glenda resides in Texas. She is a loving mother of three and grandmother of eight beautiful children. She is an active member at her local church serving as a volunteer in various ministries. Her favorite scripture is Jeremiah 29:11 *"For I know the plans I have for you. Plans to prosper you and not to harm you, plans to give you hope and a future."*

ABOUT THE AUTHOR

Evangelist Jackie Stamps

Evangelist Jackie Stamps is 48 years old and loves God! She is from Anniston, Al. She is a Minister of God's Holy Word. She is married to the love of her life Minister Scottie Stamps, for 22 Blessed years. They have three wonderful children, Brittney 29, Anthony 28, & Kadedra 24 and one beautiful granddaughter Gabrielle 10. She is a Gospel Recording Artist. The Founder of *"Virtuous Women of God Ministries"* and Founder of *"Jackie Stamps Ministries."* One of her favorite motivational scriptures is found in Romans 8:28 KJV, *"And we know that all things work together for good to them that love God, to them who are the called according to his purpose."*

Jackie's earnest desire and greatest goal is to do her best. She believes that through God it will work out for her good. She and her husband are the owners of *Blessed Hands Inc*, where he creates wood furniture made by hand- and she creates Tutus, and digitally de and more! She is the host of Mid-Day Praise w/ Evangelist Jackie on FB Live. You can find her live each Monday, Wednesday and Friday. Her husband joins her on Wednesday's.

She is also a newly published author of her first solo book titled, *"Sandpapered."* This book was sent by God to help women heal, and to let them know there is life after spiritual death.

Evangelist Stamps loves God, her family and serving His people.

ABOUT THE AUTHOR

Shagaina Clark

Shagaina Clark is an aspiring author, born December 25, 1979 in the small town of Lebanon TN. She lived with her mother and older brother where she endured various hardships and suffered through many humbling experiences. Despite the trials she faced during the early years of her life, Shagaina graduated from Lebanon High School May 1998. She did not pursue a career immediately after graduation. Instead, she worked various jobs in hopes that these jobs would lead her to her calling in life. She went through a period of drug and alcohol abuse and in the year 2000, she became pregnant with her first child. During this period of her life, Shagaina attended Tennessee Technology Center, where she graduated December 19th, 2001.After the third child was born, Shagaina became determined to create a better life for herself and her beautiful girls, Inashja, Makyah, and KeMaria. She attended church and became an Assistant Sunday School teacher. She was baptized and filled with the Holy Spirit in October 2005. Shagaina discovered her passion for working with mentally challenged people in April 2008. Working with this population of people has given her great joy. She hopes to one day become owner of an organization that caters to the need of the mentally disabled, in efforts of improving their quality of life. Shagaina began her writing journey in 2009. She loves writing poetry and is in the process of producing her first play based off her children's book, "Holey Moley", published in 2017. Shagaina is currently employed at Associated Pathologists, where she has worked for five years. She is a humble woman of God who loves traveling and meeting different people. She hopes to inspire wayward women with her testimony of the Redemptive Love of Christ. She is available and always willing to go wherever the will of God shall lead.

ABOUT THE AUTHOR

Jackqueline Mondo - Apinyi
International Contributing Author
United Kingdom

Jackqueline is a married mother to four lovely children, two of which have special needs. Jackqueline serves on the Evangelism and ushering teams at church. She also completed a practical Ministry course. She is full of passion to encourage women who have been through emotionally traumatic experiences. As Jackqueline was personally healed and uplifted by the Lord she founded *Woman and Arise and be Healed*, where she shares her personal experiences to mentor and support others in healing. In the future, she also plans to share experiences in the area of Business. With work experience and an (Hons) Degree in Hospitality Management she is self-employed within service accommodations for holiday makers, groups and business travelers.

Contact Jackqueline at:
Blessedjackquelinehealingword.blogspot.com
Blessedjackqueline on YouTube
Chokacottages La Mera Shanzu
Chokacottages Ocean and City view Nyali in Kenya

ABOUT THE AUTHOR

Christy Adams

Christy Adams was born and raised in the coalfields of southern West Virginia. She moved to Tennessee in January 2018 where she felt God was calling her to do a work for Him. Christy is known for her big smile and outgoing personality. She has always been called "Sunshine" by those who know her, but she never fails to attribute that "light" to her Saviour Jesus Christ.

Christy is the author of *"Speak Life"*, a 30-day devotional that launched in July 2019. She is currently pursuing a Masters in Psychology through Liberty University and plans to get her Ph.D. in 2022. Her life-long goal is to help others to heal through the Word of God.

ABOUT THE AUTHOR

Jamilah "Beautiful" Cooper

Aside from an Author, Jamilah "Beautiful" Cooper is a mother of four, a youth mentor, a Praise & Worship leader and Youth Director at her church, and a US Army veteran. As a profession, Jamilah is an office associate with the Arts & Sciences department of the University of Alabama. Jamilah has always loved the art of the written word; writing her first book at the age of eight. Since then she has authored and published nine books of urban fiction, children's stories, poetry, and inspiration; co-authoring two others. Along with writing, her passions include anything involving creativity and art, from music production to digital design. She is also a very vocal advocate for victims of domestic violence and sexual assault. Jamilah is the CEO of WORTHIT Inc, a 501(c)(3) nonprofit mentoring organization for young women and girls. WORTHIT was created upon discovering her purpose to reach and empower young ladies through sharing her testimony. Jamilah lives by the motto "Tell your own story and no one else can tell it wrong." And despite her past, her favorite scripture is "I will bless the Lord at all times: his praise shall continually be in my mouth." Psalm 34:1

Contact Info:
Email: jcooperbowden@gmail.com
Web: www.worthit.us
FB: @werworthitgirls
IG: @worthit_girls

ABOUT THE AUTHOR

Kimberly Gore

Kimberly Gore a Nashville native, but loves to travel and is working on filling up her map of the places she dreams of going. She is a proud mother of three, who has overcome the struggles of being a single mother and ultimately having them all attend a higher level of education. She graduated from the University of Phoenix with a degree in Human Services in 2017. Kimberly was raised in a Christian home, which was where her solid foundation began. She soon realized she needed to build her own personal relationship with God, to be able to withstand the trials and tribulations that are in her path. That is where she began to tap into her purpose. Never knowing that journaling her mind, heart and soul frequently, would usher her into God's calling on her life. Kimberly's first solo book titled *"What's Next"* is scheduled to be released in the spring of 2020. Kimberly's goal as an author is to empower you to reach for your goals and become your best self. Kimberly believes her entire existence is to bring healing to women through her life experiences and lessons learned. She is open and willing to be used in whatever capacity God directs. She believes being humble and willing. She feels this will take you farther than you could ever imagine.

Jeremiah 29:11
"For I know the plans I have for you," declares the LORD, "plans to prosper you and not to harm you, plans to give you hope and a future."

Contact Kimberly L. Gore:
KIMBERLYLASHEA.ORG
Kimberly.gore01@gmail.com
615-579-0508 (cell)

ABOUT THE AUTHOR

Elder Janice Blackmon

Elder Janice Blackmon was raised in Flint Michigan and has always had a love for God. In 2011 she became a licensed member of the Clergy, and one year later, in 2012, she was selected to go before an Ordination Council at Cornerstone Full Gospel Baptist Church where she became ordained as an Elder. She recently held the position of the International Lead Intercessor for the Theta Phi Sigma Christian Sorority Inc, a non-profit organization that seeks to uplift women in their specific gifts. Elder Blackmon's mantle is in the area of Intercession and when called upon to do so she leads the people of God into the presence of God through prayer and exaltation.

Elder Blackmon's additional teaching and training responsibilities include having taught on subjects such as "The Importance of Having an Effective Praise and Worship Team" which was presented to the music ministry of the Weeping Mary Baptist Church of Tuscaloosa. In 2014, Elder Blackmon became a recording artist with The Cornerstone Full Gospel Baptist Church Choir as the lead singer on their single entitled "Hold On."

She is the President of the Thessalonians Upsilon Chapter of Theta Phi Sigma Christian Sorority Inc, and co-founder of the *31:10 Christian Women's Book Club*. While pursuing her Doctorate with the Apostolic Institute of Higher Learning, she also serves as an instructor. In 2015 she, alongside her husband Elder Shawn Blackmon founded Blackmon and Blackmon Ministries where their focus is teaching others on "Bridging the Generational Gap in Worship". They reside in Tuscaloosa Alabama with their three collegiate children.

ABOUT THE AUTHOR

Janel Andrews

Janel Andrews is a native of Atlanta, Georgia. She currently resides in Des Moines Iowa. She is a mother of two and grandmother of one granddaughter. She is the daughter of the late Rev. Dr. Horace E. Andrews of Mt. Ephraim Baptist Church. She has held membership in various organizations such as Order of Easter Star, Theta Phi Sigma, and she was PTA president of W.E. Boyd Elementary School in Atlanta and has given back to the community by supporting her dad in feeding the homeless, visiting the sick and elderly in nursing homes and high rises throughout Atlanta. She served as CEO of the NIAA Scholarship Foundation from 2009 to 2010, and as an advocate for Alzheimer's, lupus and the Go Red for Women foundation. For years, she assisted many displaced youth in her community that varied in age of whom she loves dearly. She loves to read, travel and spend time with her friends and family.

ABOUT THE AUTHOR

Tonya S. Jackson

Tonya S. Jackson is a graduate of Louisiana Tech University, Ruston, LA with a BA degree in Journalism. After graduating college, she became the News Editor for a local newspaper. While working in the day, Tonya decided to go back to school and pursue her certification as a Medical Coder. She completed the program through Northwestern State University and LaMar Salter Technical College. Tanya is currently a Professional Certified Medical Coder and interim supervisor for the federal government at Bayne Jones Army Community Hospital at Fort Polk, LA. She also has a home business as a Contract Medical Coder. In May 2018, she answered the call on becoming a member of Theta Phi Sigma Christian Sorority, Inc. where she serves on the National Community Service Team. Jackson is also the author of two books: *"What Doesn't Break You, Motivates You"* and *"If it Doesn't Break You, it Keeps you."*

Her favorite scripture is Romans 8:28, *"And we know all things work together for good to those who love God, to those who are the called according to his purpose."*

ABOUT THE AUTHOR

Minister Charlotte Walker

Minister Charlotte Satcher-Walker is a native of DeRidder, La. She is a Servant of God called to preach and teach, mentor, and provide resources through assessing the needs of others to help change lives by teaching life skills necessary for daily living to those who are not as fortunate. She has accepted Christ calling her to walk in the full authority of God in the anointed capacity that He has purposed for her life. She's the wife of Minister Alvin J. Walker, Sr. She is active in her church Women's Mission Union and other ministries within her church. Minister Walker is willing to serve wherever there is a need. She is the Founder of *Hands of Faith Outreach Ministries* and a female Gospel group The Heavenly Voices. She is a Mother & grandmother and very family oriented. She is a member of Mt. Canaan Baptist Church in DeRidder, La under the leadership of Pastor L.F. Guy. She authored and self-published two books, "Embracing the Intimacy of Loving You and Others Too" and "Embracing a Closer Walk with God."She works for the State of Louisiana IMCAL which serves five parishes in the area of prevention to change community norms in the area of alcohol and drugs using data and evidence based practices. Minister Charlotte received her Master of Criminal Justice degree from Purdue Global University. She is continuing to pursue her Doctorate degree in Public Policy and Administration with a concentration in Criminal Justice and Philosophy. Charlotte takes nothing for granted and knows that God makes ALL THINGS POSSIBLE because without Him she could do nothing! She says the most important choice that she has accomplished is accepting Jesus Christ as her Lord and Savior and her relationship with Him. A favorite scripture that she reads daily is Psalm 91:1-4.
To expound on the last verse: if God has you under His wings, He covers you from the snares of the world. This means we just need to trust Him and know that we're safe in His arms!

ABOUT THE AUTHOR

Charmaine Witherspoon

Charmaine Witherspoon is an African American, Christian author. She currently holds degrees in both Sociology and Social Work. She is passionate about the field of addictions and helping the homeless population. She is currently working on a scholarship program for students who are passionate about the field of mental health. She hopes to one day start her own Emergency homeless shelter and recovery center. Charmaine has also created the Love yourself luncheon in which she tailors to meet the needs of the attendees. She is a member of Theta Phi Sigma Christianity Sorority, Inc. Charmaine attends Kingdom in the Valley Christian Church in Phoenix, AZ.

ABOUT THE AUTHOR

Marlo Eggerson

Marlo Lawson Eggerson hails from Racine, Wisconsin. She now resides in Amarillo, Texas. She is the wife of Darryl Eggerson and together, they have four sons. Marlo grew up in a home where her mother taught her brother, sister, and she that God is ALWAYS faithful. That teaching is something Marlo carries with her daily on her job as a Medical Assistant for over 25 years. One of the things that Marlo thanks God for is Redemptive Word Church, where she and her husband serve as Marriage Ministry Leaders. Eggerson states that she absolutely loves Sunday School and learning more about our Lord and Savior. One of her favorite quotes is "I love the Lord because He first loved me."

ABOUT THE AUTHOR

Angela Foster

Angela Foster is a woman of deep and tenacious faith in God. Angela responds to God's love with purposeful obedience to fulfill His desire for her life. She is a Warrior, an Avenger of the innocent and defender of righteousness. Her greatest desire is to challenge others to experience the love of God in their walk of faith, while overcoming the strongholds of this life. Angela's gift for asking the hard questions to promote deep thinking, leading to freedom from spiritual bondage, has led her to earn a Certificate in Life Coaching from Light University. She is currently pursuing her certification in Christian Life Coaching from Christian Leaders Institute. Angela is an up and coming entrepreneur with two marketplace ministries in the making. Her journey over the last few years has compelled her to share what she believes is the secret of spiritual warfare and victory from James 4:7, *"Submit to God. Resist the devil and he will flee."*
Angela is the mother of four amazing adult children, LaNoya, Angel, Leah, and Landon Jr. who are the joy of her life next to Jesus.

ABOUT THE AUTHOR

Keywana Wright

Keywana Wright is a native of Flint, Michigan. She is a devoted mother of one daughter, Miss Tayler Williams. Ms. Wright is a self-publisher and author of the four short devotional books, Walking in God's Destiny, Keywana's Collection of Prayers and Poems, 31 daily prayers for the Virtuous woman, and One leap into your God-Given purpose. She is a motivational speaker, writer, and prayer warriors. She hosts 5 Minutes Words of Encouragement on Facebook lives on Friday's mornings. A podcast program "Good Night Prayers with Keywana Wright" on Tuesday's at 9pm. Keywana is a Jr. Missionary and serves in various capacities at her local church as well as the community.
Keywana's dream is to work and serve in full-time women's outreach ministry. She has a God-giving love for women and to help them reach their purpose in the Kingdom of God. She believes in the power of prayer. She is a witness that there is nothing impossible to him that believe. Over the past 14 years she has continued to work in the Human Service Field. She also has worked with domestic Violence and sexual assault victims. She is a volunteer at Carriage Town Ministries. She encourages and uplifts the women at Carriage Town with her mentor, Minister Brittany Willingham. Keywana is certified as a Life coach and holds a Bachelor of Arts degree in Family Life Education from Spring Arbor University. She has a certificate in Leadership in Ministry. She continues to work in women's ministry in her local church and outreach ministry. Her favorite bible verse is found in Proverbs 3:6:
"In all thy ways acknowledge him and he shall direct thy path."

ABOUT THE AUTHOR

Jonetta Baggett

Jonetta White-Baggett is an anointed woman of God and a cheerleader for Jesus Christ. She is a devoted wife, caring mother, and a sister-friend to many. Jonetta is the owner and creator of *Uniquely-U Boutique, LLC.* Through her services, she inspires the individuality and beauty within each and every woman she encounters. Baggett believes that all women are beautiful; no matter their shape, size or skin color. Jonetta is a member of Theta Phi Sigma Christian Sorority Incorporated where her chapter is none other than the Nehemiah Nu chapter of Oxford Ms., affectionately known as "The New Nu." Jonetta currently holds the title of *Mrs. Pink* of Theta Phi Sigma Christian Sorority, Inc. and her platform is to help the less fortunate and advocacy against abuse. Jonetta is a fun, easy going spirit. She loves to encourage, inspire and push others towards their ordained purpose.

A personal quote from Jonetta Baggett:

"Your Opinion matters to you. When I think of life and what it has to offer, I think of the who's, what's and how's of life. Who will I meet along the way that we will both be able to inspire one other to be better? What is my purpose when I wear the many hats that I own? How does GOD see me while doing all of the above?"

For Uniquely U-Boutique merchandise
Contact Jonetta Baggett at:

www.uniquelyu.online

ABOUT THE AUTHOR

Lady Angela Lucas

Angela Lucas is a native of Valdosta, GA. She is the second oldest of five siblings. She is the mother of two sons. Angela completed her education in the medical field and currently serves as a triage nurse. She has received numerous honors and individual recognition for various achievements in her established field of nursing. She also has a passion for public relations, because of her love for people. Lady Angela exemplifies class and elegance in her everyday walk with Christ as her guide. She inspires and encourages other women to help combat low self-esteem. Her motto states: "Be a designer's original do not become a cheap carbon copy!" You are built for God's best do not settle for less!" Lady Angela has served and traveled with Apostle Lundy as The National Nurse and served on the Intercessor team of The Flame of Fire Ministries. She is a member of Mt. Calvary Baptist church under the leadership of Dr. Charles Vinson, where she serves as an armor bearer and other various ministries.

Lady Angela is also is a member of Theta Phi Sigma Christian Sorority Inc., also known as The Pink Society under the leadership, Founder Jessica Cole. The goal is to bring awareness of God's love to the community, by helping women learn to value themselves. She serves as an Ambassador of the Joel Omicron Chapter in Valdosta, Ga. She is the Community Service Coordinator and the Pink Tourmaline Coordinator. She also has served as the I-Care Coordinator and is a member of the Pearls of Issachar South Atlantic Region She is a member of The Ladies of Lydia, as well as The Matrons of Destiny. She is a member of the WHO's Businesswomen of Today organization. Psalm 139:14 *"I praise you because I am fearfully and wonderfully made; marvelous are your works, and I know this very well.*

Contact Lady Angela at:
Angelface652002@yahoo.com or 229-412-1980

ABOUT THE AUTHOR

Lakisha Sewell

Mrs. LaKisha Maria Sewell is the mother of three and married to Deacon DeAndrae R. Sewell Sr. of Ralph, Alabama. She is a member of St. Peter Baptist Church where she serves as a Deaconess and Youth Advisor. Lakisha has a Master of Science in Counseling and Psychology from The University of West Alabama. Her undergraduate degrees are in Psychology and Sociology from The University of West Alabama as well. She has worked with the mental health population for 10 years. Currently, LaKisha is a Coordinator of a Rehabilitation Day Program and a CPR/EFA Instructor in Tuscaloosa, Alabama. She is the Founder and CEO of Strive Outreach. LaKisha is a co-author of *Sisters to Sisters- Daily Inspirations* and participated in a published case study on "Multiple Relationships and Therapy: When Six Degrees of Separation is Not Possible."
LaKisha has been a licensed Cosmetologist for 16 years which facilitated the desire to help people in need. She spends time volunteering, researching and coordinating many projects that consist of sickle cell anemia, breast cancer, and advocating for mental health awareness. Lakisha and her husband, DeAndrae has a mission when it comes to healthy relationships. They facilitate marriage seminars/conferences and healthy relationship classes. Lakisha's motto is: *"Why Do It Alone When We Can Do It Together?"*

ABOUT THE AUTHOR

Star Word

    Star M. Holmes-Word is a Personal Development Coach, Public Speaker, and Writer. She assists women entrepreneurs in monetizing their platforms through coaching, and innovative writing techniques. Star is instrumental in helping to develop the confidence of women who have experienced trauma by helping them create safety plans for triggered memories so that they can stay focused and impact those they are divinely connected to. Star helps women develop the confidence to move from the back of the line to the front of the line. Star is the visionary co-author of *We Are Women of Substance*. The book launched in Nashville in 2018. Star released her second anthology in the summer of 2019 called *The Healing Journey*.

    Star is a native of Philadelphia, PA. Although most of her childhood was spent in Chicago, Illinois. Star spent many years in Cedar Rapids, Iowa where she opened the first Multicultural Victim/Survivor Outreach Center in 2008 and created a new position titled Multicultural Outreach Advocate.

    Star moved into Public Speaking, Writing and Coaching in 2017, after attending the *Epic Conference*. Star has been interviewed on numerous radio shows. She has been invited to be a Brand Ambassador for The Lift Conference (Poconos), The Fierce Freedom Summit (Virginia Beach), and Spark and Hustle (ATL). Additionally, she has been a guest on several webinars. She currently resides in Nashville TN with her husband and three beautiful children.

ABOUT THE AUTHOR

Leana Jefferson

Leana M. Brackens Jefferson is CEO and founder at The Capricorn Group, Yellow Diamond Society for (Cancer survivors), True Survivors, Inc. and coordinator of the annual *Extraordinary Women* Conference in Houston, Texas. Jefferson has inspired women to embrace empowerment and change in order to live a more fulfilling life. She is committed to helping others to have a life of inspiration, victory and the ability to connect with women from all walks of life. She has been invited to speak on numerous occasions, ranging from business engagements in the world of financial stability related to real estate development, investments and management, to mortgage counseling. Additionally, she has been requested to speak at church events, conferences and retreats. She has been honored and recognized on numerous occasions for her outstanding leadership and commitment to community service, including an award for inspired women in the real estate community and Who's Who. A visual presence in Houston business and the Christian community.
Jefferson is a graduate of Milby High school. She attended the University of Houston as a business and Criminal Justice major, Tomball College and Champion School of Real Estate. In 1999 she became an entrepreneur and owner of Genesis Mortgage, Inc. and The Capricorn Group. Leana has been very successful in the sales profession. *True Survivors Independent Living Facility*, helps others with special needs in the community of health care. She is presently the Operations Manager at New Vision Community Church under new leadership. Jefferson holds a Bachelors degree and is currently fulfilling the requirements for a dual Master's and Doctorate degree in Christian studies and Theology.

ABOUT THE AUTHOR

LaKesha Perdue

LaKesha R. Perdue is a mother of three adult children, LaKesha was born and raised in the southwest suburbs of Chicago, Illinois until the age of 19. She graduated from Joliet Central High School on the early out program. LaKesha is a proud grandmother of four handsome grandsons – the oldest is age 8, a set of twins (age 3), and an infant. LaKesha is an accomplished Medical Assistant, teacher, and author. She finds her passion in the ministry of dance and motivational speaking. LaKesha resides in Atlanta, GA along with her oldest daughter and grandchildren. Lakesha ministers in dance, evangelizes and teaches preschool. It is the desire of LaKesha that her words reach the heart of every woman. Perdue would like to let women know that they can make and that they are something special.

For booking and contact:
Email: Kreney925@gmail.com
Phone: 678-754-3324
Facebook LaKesha Perdue   Instagram: lrpdue3,
LinkedIn: LaKesha Perdue

ABOUT THE AUTHOR

Erica Jackson

Erica Jackson is an African American, Christian writer and Epileptic Warrior. Erica was diagnosed with Epilepsy at the age of 13. She struggled greatly with the effects of this diagnosis as child and later as a young adult. She endured several seizures that left residual effects that threatened to alter her educational journey. She was told that high school and college may be difficult due the neurological effects on her comprehension skills. Due to her difficult diagnosis with Epilepsy, Erica found herself at the brink of suicide. But she heard the voice of God say "Jeremiah 29:11-14, which says:

"For I know the thoughts that I think toward you, saith the Lord, thoughts of peace, and not of evil, to give you an expected end. Then shall ye call upon me, and ye shall go and pray unto me, and I will hearken unto you. And ye shall seek me, and find me, when ye shall search for me with all your heart. And I will be found of you, saith the Lord: and I will turn away your captivity, and I will gather you from all the nations, and from all the places whither I have driven you, saith the Lord; and I will bring you again into the place whence I caused you to be carried away captive."

Erica learned to stand tall in her purpose and walk into her destiny like a giant. She made the decision to continue her educational journey and was accepted into Talladega College. She was crowned Miss UNCF in 2016 and 2017. Jackson made it her priority to advocate for Epilepsy Awareness on her college campus and in her community as well. In May of 2017, Erica graduated with a Bachelor of Social Work degree. Jackson is currently studying for a Master of Psychology at the Chicago School of Professional Psychology.

ABOUT THE AUTHOR

Mikayla Thompson

Mikayla Thompson is an African American writer, born April of 1998 in Nashville, TN. She is the daughter of Evangelist Tanya R. Thompson. Mikayla is a senior at Tennessee State University where she is majoring in Interdisciplinary Studies. Mikayla is a member of the TSU track and field team, where she is an award-winning NCAA thrower of the shot put, discus, hammer and weight throw. Mikayla holds multiple records and individual titles across her throwing events, including 2019 Indoor OVC Shot Put Champion with a new meet record. Mikayla is the CEO of BLAC Beauty Cosmetics where she creates natural lipsticks, glosses and other products with natural processes. She is also the owner of K Digital Designs. Thompson is also a talented make-up artist.

In 2019, she co-authored "He Loves Me Not" alongside her mother. This book tells the story of her experience as a child survivor of domestic violence. She subsequently released her first individual title called "Wise & Bountiful" followed by a personal journal called "All Her Dreams in a Journal" which are both available on Amazon. Mikayla strives to be a positive influence for women who may be suffering from low self-esteem and challenges with body image.

"I can do all things through Christ who strengthens me." Philippians 4:13

Contact Mikayla Thompson at:

YouTube: Beauty By KMUA
Instagram: Beauty.by.kmua
Email: kayth81@gmail.com

ABOUT THE AUTHOR

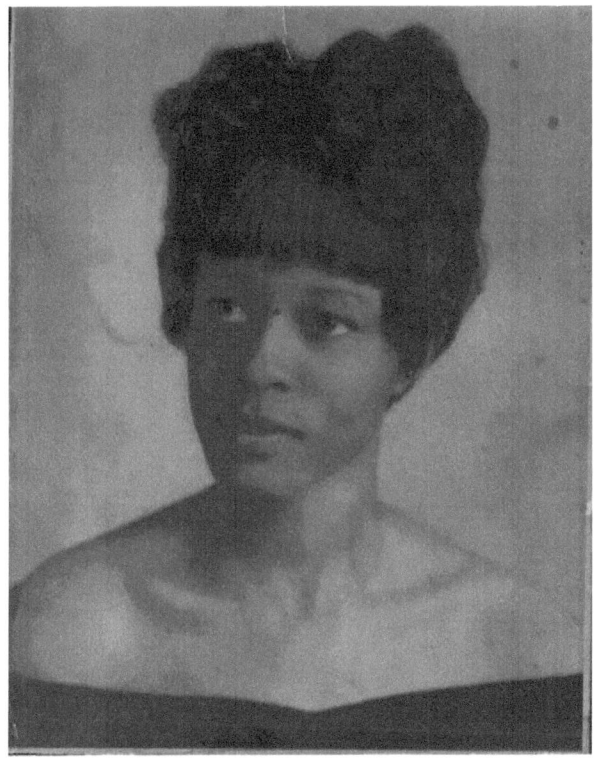

Mary Carrethers
Executive Board, Glory After the Rain Ministries

Mary Carrethers was born September 13, 1952 to the late Robert and Fannie Mai Seay. She was raised in Tuckers Crossroads, Tennessee. Mary is a 1970 graduate of Lebanon High School. She is the wife of Deacon John J. Carrethers. Mary is retired from the Comdata Corporation after more than 20 years of service. She is the mother of three children; Evangelist Tanya Thompson, LaToya Thompson and the late Johnny R. Thompson Jr. Mary is truly a General in the Faith. Her belief in God and His promises is steadfast and does not waiver.

www.ingramcontent.com/pod-product-compliance
Lightning Source LLC
Chambersburg PA
CBHW030234170426
43201CB00006B/220